David Bryan is Director of Studies and Tutor for Ordinands for Lindisfarne Regional Training Partnership, which is based in the north-east of England. He oversees the BA in Theology and Ministry, which is a degree awarded by Durham University. Before joining Lindisfarne, he was Rector of St Andrew's, Darlington. He previously taught New Testament Studies at the Queen's Foundation, Birmingham. With Professor James Crossley, he has chaired the Jesus Seminar of the British New Testament Society for many years. His previous publications include *Cosmos, Chaos and the Kosher Mentality* (1993, about to be reissued by Bloomsbury) and articles connected to Jesus studies. He is passionate about the need for fresh and imaginative approaches to Jesus, his homeland, mission and ministry.

D1628221

JESUS – HIS HOME, HIS JOURNEY, HIS CHALLENGE

A companion for Lent and Easter

David J. Bryan

First published in Great Britain in 2013

Society for Promoting Christian Knowledge
36 Causton Street
London SW1P 4ST
www.spckpublishing.co.uk

British Library Cataloguing-in-Publication Data
A catalogue record for this book is available from the British Library

ISBN 978–0–281–07108–1
eBook ISBN 978–0–281–07109–8

Typeset by Graphicraft Limited, Hong Kong
First printed in Great Britain by Ashford Colour Press
Subsequently digitally printed in Great Britain

Produced on paper from sustainable forests

Contents

Illustrations

Plates

Figure

List of illustrations

Maps

Acknowledgements

Quotations from the Mishnah are from Herbert Danby's translation (Oxford: Oxford University Press, 1933).

Quotations from Josephus are from the translation by H. St. J. Thackeray, Ralph Marcus and Louis H. Feldman in the relevant volumes of the Loeb Classical Library (Cambridge MA: Harvard University Press, 1926–8 and 1930–65).

Introduction

This book is the fruit of a ten-year gestation period! In 2001, when I was the New Testament Tutor and Director of Studies at the Queen's Foundation in Birmingham, I took the opportunity to visit Israel. I stayed at the Tantur Ecumenical Institute for four weeks, from mid-February. My hope was to use the field trip as a spur to writing a contribution to Jesus studies. Originally I was going to be accompanied by Wendy, my wife, and Isaac, our youngest child, who was about a year old. However, the political situation became unstable once more in the months leading up to our visit. In the autumn, the Prime Minister of Israel, Ariel Sharon, had encroached on what was sacred space for Muslims by entering the compound of the Al Aqsa Mosque during the Feast of Tabernacles. The period of hope that followed the Oslo Accord abruptly ended, and the second intifada began. By the time I was due to fly out in February, news bulletins spoke almost daily of suicide bombings, and we were tempted to withdraw altogether. However, the rector of Tantur, Fr Michael McGarry, reassured me that it was safe to come. We decided it was best for me to go alone. This proved to be a good decision, even if it was a disappointment at first.

Tantur occupies a liminal, strategic and significant place. It sits on a rocky ridge looking in one direction to Bethlehem and in the other to Jerusalem. Being there in 2001 was, as one may imagine, challenging and life-changing – it would be a long time before I could settle again to the normality of life in Britain. Indeed, I still cannot attend a fireworks display in November without remembering the exchange of machine-gun fire and the shells falling in Beit Jala close to Tantur. So it was not really surprising that I was unable to find the stillness needed to write when I returned to Britain. This was not helped by the significant changes in my circumstances. Not long after returning I was back in the maelstrom of a final term in the academic year at Queen's. It also proved to be my last at the Foundation. By the end of July we were settling into life in a parish in the North East, St Andrew's Church, Haughton-le-Skerne, in Darlington. My feet scarcely touched the floor for almost ten years as the challenges of a busy parish grabbed me and moved me onwards.

In the intervening years my ministry as a priest was deeply influenced both by the experience and the reflections about Jesus that had been provoked in a place of fiercely contested boundaries. But these did not find their way on to a page, at least not until 2011, when I had another opportunity to return to Tantur, now under a new rector, Fr Tim Lowe. On this occasion, although the situation on the ground in Israel and Palestine was still challenging and disturbing, Wendy and Isaac were able to join me for Holy Week and Easter. So I am very grateful that I at last have managed to complete this work. It is, however, somewhat different from the book I originally set out to write. My hope is that the depth of experience that underlies it shines through and proves to be an inspiration to you.

I would like here to acknowledge the support of the many people who made possible the two visits to the 'Holy Land' and encouraged me with the project of writing this book. I am grateful to those who helped with the award of grants, particularly the Dioceses of Birmingham and Durham, the Ecclesiastical Insurance Group and the Church of England's Council for Mission. Second, I thank my former colleagues and the Christian communities at the Queen's Foundation and St Andrew's Haughton-le-Skerne, both for allowing me time out to undertake this project and for their reflections on the ideas as they began to emerge.

To go alone to Israel in 2001 felt like the most risky and dangerous thing I had ever done, so I cannot speak too highly of the welcome and guidance I received from the various staff members at Tantur at the time, and also in the subsequent visit ten years later. I must also thank Stephen Cherry, Director of Ministerial Development in Durham Diocese, for his support before and after the study leave. He it is who suggested the title of the book. To my mind it not only sums up well the thrust of the book but also invites you to journey with me as I try to follow Jesus on his own pilgrimage. The Jesus that I feel drawn to is someone who was and is willing to cross the lines in minds and hearts that separate people from God and one another. He continues to be a source of inspiration and challenge to me.

Finally, I am thankful that I do not have to try to follow him alone. So I dedicate this book to those who have travelled with me and do so today:

> To my family: Wendy; Helga and Philip; Isaac; Hannah, Mike, Gabriella and Reuben; Joshua, Diane, Laura and Rowan;
> To the Church Family at St Andrew's, Haughton-le-Skerne;
> To my colleagues and the students at Lindisfarne Regional Training Partnership.

David J. Bryan

1

Jesus: his home

————◆◆————

Introduction

Throughout the Gospels Jesus is identified as Jesus of Nazareth (Mark 1.24). This might seem obvious to us but it is actually very surprising that someone who came to be seen by his followers as the Christ or Messiah should be so closely associated with what was then a tiny village in Lower Galilee. In view of the stories about his birth in Bethlehem, we might have expected him to be remembered as Jesus of Bethlehem. Equally, given that he was not a prominent public figure until his baptism when he was about 30 years old (Luke 3.23), we might have expected him to become known as Jesus of Capernaum, which seems to have become his main base during the years of his public ministry. But not so: he was known as Jesus of Nazareth. How are we to respond to this? Was it significant? Was it an association that arose from his long connections with the village that he could never quite shake off?

Matthew and Luke both knew that Jesus was raised in Nazareth but they both wanted to say to us that there was more to this Nazarene than met the eye. So they told stories that relate how Jesus was born in Bethlehem, the birthplace of King David (1 Sam. 16) and the location from which an ancient prophet said a future, royal messianic figure would come (Mic. 5.2–4). Plainly Matthew and Luke wanted us to understand that Jesus came to fulfil the hopes and dreams surrounding the long-since defunct royal house (cf. Matt. 1.1–17; 1.20; Luke 1.27, 32; 2.4, 11). Their accounts of how his birth took place In Bethlehem are markedly different, and so are their explanations of how he came to be known as Jesus of Nazareth.

If you were to read Matthew's story of Jesus' birth without reference to Luke's, you would have the distinct impression that Bethlehem was the home base for Joseph and Mary (see Matt. 1—2). When the magi visit the family to pay homage to Jesus, they call upon them 'in the house' – we might say, 'at home' (Matt. 2.11).

Matthew narrates how King Herod came to perceive the news about Jesus' birth as a threat to his dynasty (Matt. 2.1–8). As a result of his plot to slay Jesus along with all the male children in Bethlehem who were under two years old, Joseph, Mary and Jesus flee to Egypt. When they return later to settle in the land, it is in Galilee that they make their home rather than Judea:

> Then Joseph got up, took the child and his mother, and went to the land of Israel. But when he heard that Archelaus was ruling over Judea in place of his father Herod, he was afraid to go there. And after being warned in a dream, he went away to the district of Galilee. There he made his home in a town called Nazareth, so that what had been spoken through the prophets might be fulfilled, 'He will be called a Nazorean.'   (Matt. 2.21–23)

This is the first mention of Nazareth in Matthew's account of Jesus. As with the flight to Egypt, the choice of location is not simply Joseph's. He has responded to divine guidance and sought a place far away from the threat posed by a Herodian ruler who will not welcome a new heir to David's throne. So, quiet little Nazareth is presented as an ideal hideaway for a child who is destined to rule. As is his wont, Matthew regards the decision to settle in Nazareth as having been foretold by one of Israel's ancient prophets. The only problem is that we have no idea which prophet he had in mind!

The bafflement posed by Matthew 2.23 has not stopped intrepid New Testament scholars from offering suggestions:

- Did Matthew have in mind the legislation surrounding those who made special vows of dedication to God, the so-called vow of the 'Nazirite' (Hebrew: *nazīr*)? See Numbers 6.2–8. Certainly Matthew would have considered Jesus to be especially set apart for a divine purpose, and he might here be making a play on *nazīr*. However, Jesus' lifestyle did not conform to that of the Nazirite, at least not in respect of abstaining from alcoholic drink (Matt. 11.19).
- A second possibility is that Matthew is making links with the noun used in Isaiah 11 for a messianic figure, 'the branch' (*nētser*), which would grow from the roots of the stump of Jesse, David's father (Isa. 11.1).

Obviously the second suggestion is much more promising, but quite how Matthew got from the Hebrew nouns of *nazīr* or *nētser* to the Greek *Nazōraios*, and from the latter to the Greek noun for the village, *Nazaret*, is anyone's guess. However Matthew did it, he wanted to make the point that the period of residency in Nazareth fulfilled God's purposes and plans for Jesus' life. And it was a place of safety or sanctuary away from the dangers posed to Jesus, the son of David, son of Abraham and son of God, by the rival king of the Jews, Archelaus, the son of Herod.

We turn now briefly to Luke's account of Jesus' origins. He tells us that Mary and Joseph lived in Nazareth in Galilee *before* Jesus' birth (1.26). He portrays both as having links with Judea – Mary's kinswoman Elizabeth is married to a priest who is active at the Temple in Jerusalem (1.36), and Joseph's family are evidently from Bethlehem. The latter provides the occasion for their being in Bethlehem at the time Jesus is born. They had to come south from Nazareth to take part in a census (2.1–7) and remained there for 40 days after Jesus' birth, until they had completed the purification rites required by the law (2.22–38; cf. Lev. 12.1–6). Then they 'returned to Galilee, to their own town of Nazareth' (2.39).

Luke never provides an explanation of why Joseph and Mary were living in Galilee, but it is clear that Nazareth was their home town, and the census provided a somewhat unexpected reason for their being in Bethlehem for the birth. Historians are as puzzled about Luke's claim that the whole Roman world underwent a census as they are about Matthew's account of a massacre by Herod of infants in Bethlehem, and his mysterious prophecy in the Old Testament that the Messiah 'will be called a Nazorean' (Matt. 2.23). Somehow or other they both manage to get Jesus into Bethlehem for his birth, and back to Nazareth for his emerging years towards adulthood. But you are left with the distinct feeling that it was the stubborn connection between Jesus and Nazareth that required the extra elucidation of his identity provided by their birth stories. Perhaps they were aware of the kind of pejorative attitude to Nazareth evident in the question posed by Nathaniel: 'Can anything good come out of Nazareth?' (John 1.46). Be that as it may, while their stories add another layer of mystique to the identity of Jesus, they did not dislodge the title Jesus of Nazareth from the record, and that is surely significant.

We turn now briefly to Mark. At various points in his Gospel, Jesus is referred to as Jesus of Nazareth. Mark introduces Jesus to us as an adult who comes from 'Nazareth of Galilee' to seek baptism by John in the Jordan (Mark 1.9). After his testing in the wilderness, Jesus calls the fishermen Simon and Andrew, James and John, to follow him. The location of this event is no more specific than 'along the sea of Galilee' (v. 16), but Mark must have intended us to think they were close to Capernaum (v. 21), where Simon and Andrew have a home near to the synagogue (v. 29). In a subsequent episode Mark portrays Jesus as one who does not want to be limited to one location (vv. 38–39). Even so, Mark also comes to describe Jesus as being 'at home' in Capernaum (2.1). This implies that Jesus rented a property here and that it functioned like a base camp for his public ministry (see also 3.19). But as noted above, the title Jesus of Nazareth still sticks to him like glue – indeed, it seems to be thrown in his face by the demonized man during his first visit to the synagogue in Capernaum: 'Just then there was in their synagogue a man with an unclean spirit, and he cried out, "What have you to do with us, Jesus of Nazareth?"' (1.23–24). Despite the underlying aggression, the demonized man also calls Jesus 'the Holy One of God' (v. 24). Thus this story draws our attention to the mystery at the heart of Mark's Gospel, namely that the man from Nazareth is also the Son of God.

Mark reminds us of this paradox a little later by narrating a less than successful visit by Jesus to his home town and its synagogue (6.1–6). His humble origins are underlined by the local people, who refer to Jesus as the 'carpenter'. They name members of his closest family – Mary, his mother, and James, Joses, Judas and Simon, his brothers. They also refer to his sisters, who are unnamed.

The title Jesus of Nazareth features once again in Mark as the story begins to draw to its close. It is the inspiration for an importunate plea for help as Jesus exited Jericho on his final journey to Jerusalem:

> As he and his disciples and a large crowd were leaving Jericho, Bartimaeus son of Timaeus, a blind beggar, was sitting by the roadside. When he heard that it was Jesus of Nazareth (Greek: *Iēsous ho Nazarēnos*), he began to shout out and say, 'Jesus, Son of David, have mercy on me!' (Mark 10.46–47)

The variations between Mark, Matthew and Luke are worth considering here. Matthew recounts that the crowd said, 'This is the prophet Jesus from Nazareth in Galilee' (Matt. 21.11), whereas Luke's crowds use a term very close linguistically to Matt. 2.23: 'Jesus of Nazareth (Greek: *Iēsous ho Nazōraios*) is passing by' (Luke 18.37).

The Nazareth connection of Jesus is next underlined in Mark's narration of Peter's betrayal of Jesus (Mark 14.66–72). Although

Mark does not tell us that Peter's accent gave him away (Mark 14.70; cf. Matt. 26.73), the servants of the high priest recognize that he is from Galilee, and he is accused of being 'with Jesus, the man from Nazareth' (Mark 14.67). Finally, Jesus' link to Nazareth is referred to for the last time in the story of the empty tomb on Easter Day. The young man, whom the women encounter in the tomb, announces to them:

> Do not be alarmed; you are looking for Jesus of Nazareth, who was crucified. He has been raised; he is not here. Look, there is the place they laid him. But go, tell his disciples and Peter that he is going ahead of you to Galilee; there you will see him, just as he told you. (Mark 16.6–7)

So Mark frequently reminds us that his central figure is Jesus of Nazareth. This title stresses his humble origins but is not reserved for the mouths of Jesus' antagonists. Rather it underlines the mystery that Jesus is much more than a carpenter from Nazareth. And yet he is still Jesus of Nazareth, even after his resurrection.

If Matthew and Luke address the paradox posed by Mark's Gospel by narrating stories about Jesus' birth in Bethlehem, then John takes an even larger step. For him, the origins of Jesus lie even further back at the beginning of time and creation itself.

> In the beginning was the Word, and the Word was with God, and the Word was God. He was in the beginning with God. All things came into being through him, and without him not one thing came into being. What has come into being in him was life, and the life was the light of all people. (John 1.1–4)

John places Jesus into a cosmic drama that transcends space and time. His Gospel is a story about the whole cosmos; and it is an account of how creation will be made new again. And yet John's Jesus is still very much a human being: 'And the Word became flesh and lived among us, and we have seen his glory, the glory as of a father's only son, full of grace and truth' (1.14).

Here we need to remember that the Word became Jewish flesh – 'He came to what was his own' (John 1.11) – and he is still very definitely from Nazareth. The paradoxical nature of this combination is very clearly highlighted, especially in the discussion between Philip and Nathaniel:

> Philip found Nathanael and said to him, 'We have found him about whom Moses in the law and also the prophets wrote, Jesus son of Joseph from Nazareth.' Nathanael said to him, 'Can anything good come out of Nazareth?' Philip said to him, 'Come and see.'   (John 1.45–46)

Obviously Nazareth did not feature in the list of places where one simply must live, and was certainly not supposed to be part of the *curriculum vitae* of the Messiah! This stumbling block seems to be in the background to the discussion in John 7.25–30 in which Jesus' messianic credentials are being ruled out by some because they know where he comes from.

In two more places John relates that Jesus was addressed as Jesus of Nazareth. The first is in the arrest of Jesus in the Garden:

> So Judas brought a detachment of soldiers together with police from the chief priests and the Pharisees, and they came there with lanterns and torches and weapons. Then Jesus, know-ing all that was to happen to him, came forward and asked them, 'For whom are you looking?' They answered, 'Jesus of Nazareth.' Jesus replied, 'I am he.' Judas, who betrayed him, was standing with them. When Jesus said to them, 'I am he', they stepped back and fell to the ground. Again he asked them, 'For whom are you looking?' And they said, 'Jesus of Nazareth.'
>   (John 18.2–7)

John's Jesus is content to be identified as Jesus of Nazareth, and yet his acknowledgement also comes across as almost a disclosure of his divinity – 'I am he' is an echo of 'I am', the divine name (cf. Exod. 3.14). This is underlined by the reactions of his antagonists, who fall to the ground as if they have seen an appearance of God.

Finally, it is intriguing that it is John alone who tells us that the charge nailed to the cross of Jesus included the title 'Jesus of Nazareth':

> Pilate also had an inscription written and put on the cross. It read, 'Jesus of Nazareth, the King of the Jews.' Many of the Jews read this inscription, because the place where Jesus was crucified was near the city; and it was written in Hebrew, in Latin, and in Greek. (John 19.19–20)

The other Gospels omit any reference to Nazareth in the charge – see Mark 15.26; Matt. 27.37; Luke 23.38. It is perhaps highly significant that in a Gospel that most accentuates the divinity of Jesus and understands the crucifixion as Jesus' glorification, the author should remind us that Jesus is crucified as Jesus of Nazareth.

In the light of the above survey of the Gospels, there can be no doubt that Nazareth was Jesus' home town. But does this have any significance? In what follows I am going to ask, 'What impact might the setting of Nazareth have made upon Jesus as he grew up there?' If we follow Luke's lead then we should imagine Jesus growing and developing much like any other boy. 'Yes,' Luke would say, 'he was a special child, but he was also like young Samuel' – Jesus 'grew and became strong, filled with wisdom; and the favour of God was upon him' (Luke 2.40; cf. 1 Sam. 2.26). So a journey of growth for Jesus is implicit, in which Nazareth, the close family and the community all played their part.

Here it would be worthwhile to pause briefly to reflect on the concept of our 'home town' as our *Heimat*. In German, Austrian and Swiss thought, someone's place of origin has been seen as an integral part of their identity – regional identity, along with regional dialect, was considered foundational within this concept of 'home'. This was seen as patriotic without being necessarily nationalistic. Nazi Ideology, with its emphasis on Aryan identity and the obscene linkage of 'blood' and 'soil', is now regarded as a perversion of the idea of *Heimat*. German intellectuals have rightly tried to reclaim the concept. In his *Heimat* trilogy of TV films, first shown in 1984, 1992 and 2004 respectively, Edgar Reitz, the director and writer, created a story about various families and characters who principally were based in his own homeland, the Hunsrück region in the far west of Germany. At various points in the drama key characters leave the region – but they need to come back to discover who they are. The story clearly reflected Reitz's own search for meaning and identity but perhaps points to something so many of us seek in a world that feels ever more fragmented and complicated – a place that is home and helps us make sense of who we are.

Shortly, we will ask what it was like to live in Nazareth in Jesus' day, and we will consider how Nazareth might have been *Heimat* for him. But before we do, I wonder if there are places or communities that are deeply connected with your sense of who you are?

Questions for reflection or discussion

- If someone were to describe you as *Michael of X* or *Mavis of Z*, where would that be?
- In other words, do you have a place that is your *Heimat*, a place that gives you your identity?
- How does this work and how does it impact upon your life?
- If you find this exercise difficult, what are the reasons? And how do you feel about them?

Putting Nazareth on the map

In this section we set off on a journey in search of Nazareth in the lifetime of Jesus. Can we get past the modern Nazareth to the tiny place in which Jesus' family settled? What was it like

Plate 1.1 The way to Nazareth
Source Photograph by the author.

then? How might it have shaped a young lad as he grew up there from a child into a man?

Lower Galilee, in which Nazareth lies, is characterized by several parallel east–west hill ranges (see Map 1.1). The Nazareth range is the southernmost of these higher lands. Modern Nazareth is to be found in a natural bowl that reaches from 320 metres (1,050 feet) to the crest of the hills, which are about 490 metres (1,600 feet) above sea level. If you set off to the east, after 25 km (16 miles) you will come to the Sea of Galilee, and if you head to the south-east you only need to go 9 km (5.6 miles) to come to Mount Tabor.

In the lifetime of Jesus this region was a culturally diverse Jewish territory under the rule of the Tetrarch Herod Antipas, who also reigned over Perea in the Transjordan. As villages went it was tiny! Today the modern 'city' of Nazareth is the largest Arab city in Israel, and is populated mainly by Christians. It has around 65,000 inhabitants, which is about one-third of the size of a British city like York or Oxford. The Nazareth that Jesus knew could not have been more different from that of today.

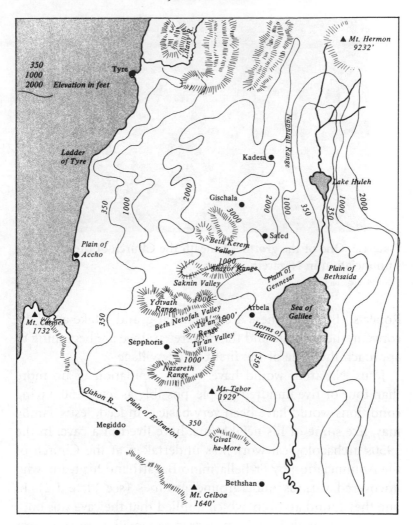

Map 1.1 Galilee: physical features

Source S. Freyne, *Galilee* (Edinburgh: T. & T. Clark, 2000), p. xviii. Used with permission.

When you stand in the modern bustling, busy place that Nazareth is today, it is really difficult to imagine what it might have been like when Jesus lived here. You get a better idea of the scale of the village if you can get sight of the lithograph prints made between 1838 and 1840 by the Scottish artist David

Plate 1.2 One of the grottoes beneath the Church of the Annunciation in Nazareth
Source Photograph by the author.

Roberts.[1] But even these are somewhat grand – take away the convent, the mosque and the minaret and we are beginning to approach the scale of the first-century village!

Jesus' Nazareth would have had a population of no more than four or five hundred people, possibly as few as 50. Living conditions would have been very basic – indeed, Jesus' family may, like some of his neighbours, have lived in a cave. In the 1950s archaeological work was undertaken at the Church of the Annunciation by Fr Bellarmino Bagatti and his team, who uncovered various underground grottoes (see Plate 1.2). In one they found an oven, which implied that the cave was once a home – though it was considered 'so small as to serve one family only'.[2]

In a recent book entitled *Holy Land?*, Andrew Mayes notes that pilgrims to the Holy Land frequently find themselves 'required to go down in to caves'. For Mayes this has profound significance:

> Many of the holy places are, in fact, caves. The pilgrim descends underground into sacred grottoes and caverns, and, in the

subterranean mystery, finds God. These hidden chambers in the bowels of the earth turn out to be liminal places, thresholds of the divine.[3]

Mayes perceptively goes on to point out that 'caves are bound up with the New Testament story':

> At Bethlehem, the focal point of devotion and pilgrimage is the cave of the nativity under Justinian's sixth-century basilica . . . The most important cave for Christians is the cave of Christ's burial and resurrection, parts of which are preserved in the *edicule* or 'little house' in the Church of Resurrection, known as the Holy Sepulchre.[4]

The Orthodox tradition of iconography has consistently repre-sented Jesus' birth as being linked to a cave. While we have no way of ascertaining whether or not Jesus was born in a cave in Bethlehem, it seems to have as much right to be taken seriously as the tradition that he was born in a stable outside an inn. Luke nowhere refers to an 'inn': he actually writes that 'there was no room in the *guest-room*' (2.7), using the Greek noun *kataluma*, a word only employed elsewhere in his Gospel for the upper room where Jesus and his followers celebrated the Passover (22.11). Luke's own preferred noun for an inn is *pandocheion* (10.34). Thus Luke seems to suggest that Joseph and Mary visited the home of a family member, and because the guest-room was occupied by other visitors for the census, a contingency arrangement was required: part of the home that was normally occupied by the family's livestock was co-opted for the use of Mary and Joseph.

Whether or not this is what happened, Mayes aptly invites us here to see the cave as a key idea for understanding Jesus. Through birth, God in Christ enters the deep dark cave of profound human need. Through the cave of death he plumbs the depths of human suffering and loss. And if Jesus' life was a journey between caves, there is something very fitting about the possibility of a cave being his home in Nazareth.

Pause to pray Psalm 130

Out of the depths I cry to you, O LORD.
  Lord, hear my voice!
Let your ears be attentive
  to the voice of my supplications!

If you, O LORD, should mark iniquities,
  Lord, who could stand?
But there is forgiveness with you,
  so that you may be revered.

I wait for the LORD, my soul waits,
  and in his word I hope;
my soul waits for the Lord
  more than those who watch for the morning,
  more than those who watch for the morning.

O Israel, hope in the LORD!
  For with the LORD there is steadfast love,
  and with him is great power to redeem.
It is he who will redeem Israel
  from all its iniquities.

Not everyone finds palatable the idea of Jesus' family home being a cave! Certainly, later in life Jesus was quite accustomed to sleeping without home comforts, and indeed once said, 'Foxes have holes, and birds of the air have nests; but the Son of Man has nowhere to lay his head' (Matt. 8.20). But living in a cave might not have been so bad as we imagine – there are modern cave dwellers in Israel/Palestine.

In 2011 I visited the Nassar family in Israel. Their home is the base of the Tent of Nations Project, which aims to promote reconciliation in Israel–Palestine. Their vision is summed up on the striking stone at the entrance to the vineyard: 'We refuse to be enemies'. The message is written in three languages – Arabic,

English and German. Behind it, inscribed in Hebrew, on a separate stone, are written the words of Psalm 133.1, 'How very good and pleasant it is when kindred live together in unity!'

Nayef Nassar, whose father Daheer purchased the land in 1916, lived in a cave on the site for more than 60 years. Located between Bethlehem and Hebron, they have found themselves embroiled in a long dispute with the Israeli government, who in 1991 declared the area, including Daheer's vineyard, state property. So far they have successfully resisted this equivalent of a compulsory purchase order, but have experienced many pressures, including the prohibition to build on the surface. Such is their determination not to be forced off the land that they are excavating more cave dwellings and other underground facilities on the site![5]

And if the idea of a home in a cave for Jesus, Mary and Joseph is still off the map for you, you might be relieved to know that caves as homes or places of residence were not the only option in Nazareth. Indeed, Bagatti, the archaeologist we noted above, felt unsure that the caves he had excavated had actually been lived in. Noting that there were no 'ashes, signs of smoke on the ceiling', he surmised that they were most likely the underground adjuncts of houses that have long gone.[6] Here we should briefly mention the more recent research undertaken by the Nazareth Village Farm Project. After four seasons of excavation, licensed by the Israel Antiquities Authority and under the joint direction of Ross Voss and Stephen Pfann, the project is confident that the site was used as 'a complete Roman Period terrace farm with a winepress, watchtowers, olive crushing stones, irrigation systems, and an ancient quarry'.[7] They also undertook to reconstruct the layout of a typical house of the period, and describe it as follows:

> Archaeological excavations of 1st Century agricultural settlements show that people usually lived in small rooms built around a central open courtyard. These houses usually began as what is called the simple house, a building subdivided into

a relatively large room (traklin) with smaller rooms for sleeping and storage. This building would be attached to an open court-yard – furnished with a water cistern and oven – where much of the domestic activities (cooking, cleaning, weaving, etc.) would take place. In regions such as Nazareth, the soft limestone bedrock was often hewn into caves and underground com-plexes ideal for storage.[8]

So for these investigators the caves would have formed just part of the homes of the people, and were their equivalent of a cool room. Even so we are still dealing with basic living conditions, an observation underlined by Craig Evans in his recent *Jesus and His World: The Archaeological Evidence.* Evans points out that the remains of homes in Nazareth reveal that they were of 'simple, rustic construction'. Neither public buildings nor paved streets have been discovered. The homes were made 'of field-stones and mud, with roofs supported by poles and overlaid with reeds and mud'.[9] And as far as we can tell, there was no adornment such as mosaics or frescoes.

What did it feel like to live in these conditions?

Read the following views of some of the experts on Nazareth and Galilee and then tackle the questions for reflection or discussion below.

Sean Freyne

life within the village confines was far from idyllic. Dwellings were small and clustered together, and generally, living con-ditions must have been primitive, giving rise to frequent illness and a short life-expectation. Attacks from passing robbers and highwaymen were frequent, explaining the location of some of the more remote settlements – away from the road and high up on the slopes of the hills. Invading armies were also frequent sources of harassment, as the villagers were compelled to make provisions available, irrespective of their own needs. In this regard Galilee . . . had more than its fair share.[10]

Under Herod Antipas, Galilee enjoyed a long period of relative calm, so these harsh realities may have been tempered a little. Again, Freyne offers a fascinating perspective:

> Antipas did bring definite stability to Galilee and cushioned it from some . . . of the harsh realities of village existence elsewhere. What we encounter, rather, are the petty squabbles of neighbours who sow weeds among each other's wheat, or small-town animosities . . . Villagers generally shared such communal facilities as wells, olive presses, threshing floors and baking ovens, it would seem, but these could easily give rise to local dissensions rather than fostering community spirit.[11]

Jonathan Reed

Reed, who has also written widely about the archaeology of Galilee, concurs in a recent article with Freyne's bleak picture.

> life in first-century Galilee . . . cannot be characterized as stable. Chronic and seasonal disease, especially malaria, cut down significant segments of the population and left even the healthy quite often ill. The age structure was youthful, women bore many children, random death made family and household patterns ephemeral, young men were often mobile, and elderly women especially vulnerable. Survival depended on extended family networks, especially for the most vulnerable, old women and young children.[12]

Reed regards the challenges in respect of health and life expectancy as a significant factor in causing Galilee under Antipas to be demographically unstable, with a lot of people moving from place to place, from village to city, especially with the construction of Sepphoris and Tiberias. However, Reed considers that one's life expectancy would not have been improved by such moves. Malaria was a problem in and around Galilee, and standing water is the breeding ground for the anopheles, the mosquitoes, that carry the disease. Cities like Sepphoris and Tiberias collected water in cisterns and therefore increased the risks. The other factor to bear in mind is height: the anopheles disappear above 1,500 metres. So if you wanted to move to a city in Galilee, Sepphoris was safer than Tiberias; and if you wanted to stay in a village setting, Nazareth and Cana were safer than villages like Capernaum and Magdala.[13]

Questions for reflection or discussion

- How do you respond to these two descriptions of life in first-century Galilee?
- How significant do you think it is that it was tiny Nazareth where Jesus was nurtured and grew up?
- How do you think growing up in Nazareth might have shaped and influenced Jesus in his later life?
- What are your perspectives on the 'small' place?
- Are there any advantages in viewing the world from relative obscurity?

Nazareth and Sepphoris

Nazareth lay just 3–4 miles (6 km) from Sepphoris, the major city of Galilee at the turn of the Era. It strategically overlooked the Beit Netofa valley, upon which it depended for its subsistence (see Plate 1.3).

In Jesus' childhood, Sepphoris became part of the tetrarchy of Antipas. According to Josephus, the city had been captured by the Romans and burned during the troubles that had erupted when Herod died in 4 BCE.[14] Antipas embarked on a major rebuilding programme sometime between 4 BCE and 12 CE, and made the city his administrative headquarters, the 'ornament of all Galilee',[15] at least until he built his new capital on the shore of Lake Galilee, which he named Tiberias to honour the new emperor Tiberius.[16] Richard Horsley points out that this development signalled a significant political change for the Galileans. They were:

Plate 1.3 The Beit Netofa valley, viewed from the south-west of Sepphoris
Source Photograph courtesy of Todd Bolen/BiblePlaces.com.

no longer under the political jurisdiction of the Temple and high priesthood in Jerusalem ... Suddenly ... most Galileans, who had been ruled from distant capitals before, now experienced one of those 'royal' capitals as an immediate presence, within view and only a half-day's walk away.[17]

Sepphoris was a city of between 12,000 and 15,000 people. What kind of city was it? A few years ago Richard Batey, in his *Jesus and the Forgotten City*, interpreted the city very much as a cosmopolitan, typical Graeco-Roman city, replete with Roman arches, a theatre and a mix of Gentile and Jewish population, each following their own religious practices. He then went on to argue that Jesus had been deeply influenced by this city and its culture.[18]

Archaeological studies of Sepphoris have been very intense since the 1970s and are still ongoing.[19] The difficulties lie in correctly identifying the periods at which the Graeco-Roman features were introduced. The emerging consensus is that these belong to a later period than Batey had allowed, after the destruction of Jerusalem in 70 CE when the political situation was radically different. The Sepphoris of Antipas' tetrarchal rule was manifestly a Jewish city in which 'the Jewish faith and lifestyle were taken seriously'.[20] In the excavation of the city dump, for example, archaeologists identified a layer of destruction that is plausibly connected to the major war of 70 CE. Above that layer the pig bones 'represent 30 per cent of the animal remains', and below that layer there are none.[21] So pork was not on the menu in Sepphoris prior to the First Jewish War. The other telltale signs of a predominantly Jewish culture are the many fragments of stone vessels that were used for cooking and drinking, and the ritual bathing pools (see below). Both attest a concern to follow a life of ritual purity.

Sepphoris in this period included a quarter in which aristocratic Jews lived in well-proportioned houses along the street (see Plate 1.4). Their homes all seem to have had a mod-con of the first century, namely their own *miqveh* or ritual bath, which not only meant they were people who cared about ritual

Plate 1.4 The excavations of the first-century Jewish city of Sepphoris

Source Photograph courtesy of Todd Bolen/BiblePlaces.com.

purity but also that they had no need to go to a communal bath before public worship.

All of the villages of western Lower Galilee were ruled and taxed from Sepphoris, so the silence in the Gospels about Jesus ever visiting Sepphoris is deafening. The same is true of the other major urban development, Tiberias, constructed by Antipas and founded in 18 CE while Jesus still lived at home.

Here we need to think about Jesus' father, Joseph, who was described as a carpenter: 'Is not this the carpenter's son? Is not his mother called Mary? And are not his brothers James and Joseph and Simon and Judas?' (Matt. 13.55). As we noted earlier, in Mark's account it is Jesus himself who is the 'carpenter' rather than Joseph. The title 'carpenter' (Greek: *ho tektôn*) probably referred to someone who worked on a range of tasks that included the manufacture and repair of furniture and farm equipment, the joinery in home construction, and possibly extended to working with stone as well as wood.

The fact that Joseph and Jesus are each referred to as a *tektôn* tells us something about the social status of their family. Unlike farmers they would not have had land to till and maintain. This implies that somewhere in the past they had lost their land and that they therefore had to survive by plying a trade. Although Nazareth was their home base, they may have needed to be peripatetic in terms of seeking gainful employment, which may explain why they were living in Galilee in the north rather than Bethlehem, the village associated with Joseph's family in the infancy narratives (Matt. 1—2; Luke 1—2).

Intriguingly *The Miracle Maker*, the 2002 film animation directed by Derek W. Hayes and Stanislav Sokolov, begins with Jesus working as a construction worker in Sepphoris. It perhaps portrays the city as a little too Roman, but you might like to watch the first scene, 'No Cure'. It is reminiscent of Fred Flintstone leaving work for the weekend: Jesus is saying farewell to his workmates as he sets out to discover his vocation as the son of God – brilliant film work, to be sure, which helps children

21

(and adults!) connect Jesus to something they can understand. Murray Watts, the screenwriter, was clearly clued up about the close proximity of Nazareth and Sepphoris, and his speculation seems reasonable: Jesus – and presumably Joseph before him – could hardly have ignored the opportunities for work granted by Antipas' civic projects in Sepphoris.

But the stubborn fact remains that Jesus is not described in the Gospels as ever visiting Sepphoris after his public ministry began. Why is that? Three explanations have been offered:

1 The Gospels do not mention it because Jesus was not success-ful there (the view taken by D. W. Bösen).
2 Jesus did not go there because he was savvy enough to learn from what happened to John the Baptist, and avoided the two cities where the Herodians were dominant (the view taken by Sean Freyne).
3 Jesus did not go there because it was a city with different social and religious traditions from those of the villages in Galilee (the view taken by Gerd Theissen and Annette Merz).

All three sound possible, but we will probably never know fully why Jesus is not connected to Sepphoris. What we can say is that it must have been a very different place from wee, tiny Nazareth – and as we shall see in later chapters, this diversity is just the tip of the iceberg as far as the world of Jesus went.

Questions for reflection or discussion

- Try and place the three explanations offered above in order of likelihood.
- Can you think of any other explanations?
- Where are the places and communities close to you that you never visit? Why is that?
- Do you have any sense of calling to engage with the people of those places?

2
Jesus: his journey (part 1)

—•◦•—

Introduction

Luke paints a picture of the Holy Family making an annual pilgrimage to Jerusalem in the south for the Feast of the Passover.

> Now every year his parents went to Jerusalem for the festival of the Passover. And when he was twelve years old, they went up as usual for the festival. When the festival was ended and they started to return, the boy Jesus stayed behind in Jerusalem, but his parents did not know it. Assuming that he was in the group of travellers, they went a day's journey. Then they started to look for him among their relatives and friends. When they did not find him, they returned to Jerusalem to search for him. After three days they found him in the temple, sitting among the teachers, listening to them and asking them questions. And all who heard him were amazed at his understanding and his answers. When his parents saw him they were astonished; and his mother said to him, 'Child, why have you treated us like this? Look, your father and I have been searching for you in great anxiety.' He said to them, 'Why were you searching for me? Did you not know that I must be in my Father's house?' But they did not understand what he said to them. Then he went down with them and came to Nazareth, and was obedient to them. His mother treasured all these things in her heart.   (Luke 2.41–51)

In this chapter we are going to try and imagine what it would have been like to make such a journey in the first century. You will find it helpful to kindle your imagination by doing one or both of the following:

23

- Watch Scene 2, 'My Beloved Son', of the animated film *The Miracle Maker* discussed in Chapter 1, and note down the things that stand out for you from this reconstruction of the visit of the 12-year-old Jesus to Jerusalem with his family.
- Luke's story also caught the imagination of the pre-Raphaelite artist William Holman Hunt, who painted his famous *The Finding of the Saviour in the Temple* in 1854–5, after his first visit to Jerusalem. This can be viewed today in Birmingham Museum and Art Gallery, or online.[1] Spend a few minutes studying Hunt's painting, alongside the story from Luke's Gospel above.

Questions for reflection or discussion

- What strikes you about the painting?
- What feelings or thoughts does it evoke?
- How does Hunt represent the teachers and scribes?
- What is happening with Mary?
- What do you make of the posture or comportment of Jesus as Mary attempts to embrace him?
- Where is Joseph, and what do you imagine he is thinking?

Pilgrimage from Galilee to Jerusalem

The description of a great group of people travelling together strikes a chord in us. It is not hard to conjure up in the mind the picture of such a caravan walking to Jerusalem, perhaps with a couple of beasts of burden to carry the baggage, sleeping at night under the stars around a camp fire. And one can easily imagine the excitement of such a trip for a group from a tiny village like Nazareth.

They went because the Law of Moses required it. According to Exodus 23.14–17 and Deuteronomy 16.16, males were required to attend three major pilgrim festivals in the year.

- The Feast of the Passover, also known as the 'festival of un-leavened bread', which was celebrated in the month of Abib – that is, early spring. It lasted a week and was associated with the nation's exodus from Egypt.
- The Feast of Weeks, also known as Pentecost, because it was 50 days after the Passover. It was a short celebration of one day, and included the presentation of the first fruits of the grain harvest.
- The Feast of Tabernacles or Booths, which was celebrated at the end of the agricultural year – that is, the autumn. It was also known as 'the feast of ingathering', and was a cele-bration of the grape harvest and also had connections with the wilderness wanderings. Pilgrims were expected to reside in temporary or makeshift shelters for a week.

In this light, Luke presents us with the picture of a faithful Jewish family who made it their business to go together to celebrate the Passover in Jerusalem. That said, it is inter-esting he does not mention the expectation that Joseph and Jesus should turn up for Pentecost and Tabernacles as well!

When they went to the festivals, did the people of Nazareth travel together? Did everyone always go? Were old people and pregnant or nursing mothers exempted? How old did children have to be before they were expected to go? How often would Galileans like Jesus' family have journeyed south to Jerusalem for the pilgrim festivals?

Questions like these were complicated both by geography and also by the political landscape of the day. Joseph, Mary, Jesus and their family would have had two main options in terms of route to Jerusalem (see Map 2.1 overleaf). Neither can be described as a stroll in the park or a ramble in the countryside.

Option 1 was the shortest distance, and meant going through the territory of Samaria:

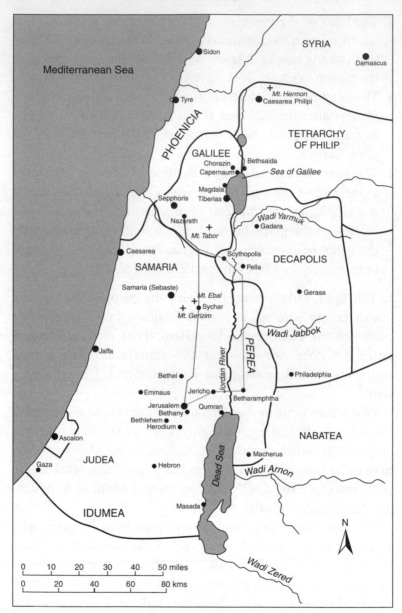

Map 2.1 The political map and pilgrims' pathways from Nazareth to Jerusalem early in the first century CE

- Stage 1: south from Nazareth into Samaria, stopping somewhere near Shechem (Sychar in John 4.5) (approximately 66 km or 41 miles).
- Stage 2: from Shechem to Taybeh (Ephraim in John 11.54) (approximately 52 km or 32 miles).
- Stage 3: from Taybeh to Jerusalem (approximately 36 km or 22 miles).

By this route they would have walked approximately 154 km or 95 miles.

Option 2 was longer but had the not insignificant advantage of avoiding the territory of the Samaritans. It would have gone something like this:

- Stage 1: south from Nazareth to the Decapolis, probably via Scythopolis (approximately 37 km or 23 miles).
- Stage 2: from Scythopolis, east across the Jordan into Perea, and then south along the Jordan valley to a point close to Jericho (approximately 105 km or 65.25 miles).
- Stage 3: west to Jericho, and finally up the steep and narrow pass to Jerusalem (approximately 54 km or 33.5 miles).

By this route the pilgrimage would have entailed a journey of approximately 196 km or 121.75 miles.

How long would such journeys have taken? The Confraternity of St James, who help pilgrims on the famous trail from Camino to Santiago in Spain, advise that stronger and fitter people can manage 30 km per day in Spanish conditions.[2] If their advice was followed by Jesus' family, then by following Option 1 they would have been on the road for about five days, and by following Option 2 for six to seven days. Given that the Passover itself lasted a week, that would mean that the festival would have taken up the best part of three weeks, including the journeys.

So pilgrimages would have involved huge expense in terms of gifts to present to God, the requisite costs of board and lodging and, most of all, the loss of earnings. They also inevitably entailed dangers and challenges, as we shall see. So it must be doubtful whether a poor family like Jesus' could have done this more than once a year. Indeed, scholars such as Richard Horsley have suggested that the Galileans of Jesus' day would not have felt obligated to attend the festivals as frequently as the Law required. Horsley makes his case on the basis of the independence of Galileans from Judeans and the complicated history of the relationship between them.[3] However, we should not doubt that in Jesus' day the Jewish people of Galilee felt bonds of loyalty to the Temple. Nor should we understate the importance of the festivals as a means of lifting the spirits of those who undertook them, especially the poor. Sean Freyne has astutely expressed this as follows:

> life in a Galilean village was never easy and sometimes brutal, constantly under pressure from above, usually from city-based people that threatened to deprive the less fortunate of the necessities of life, thus reducing them to penury. Enjoyment was confined to the odd visit of a wandering minstrel or the religious festival. Though fraught with danger, the pilgrimage to Jerusalem must have had a very definite social function for Galilean Jewish peasants, lifting them temporarily out of the narrow confines of village life and bestowing a sense of belonging to something greater.[4]

Questions for reflection or discussion

- Have you experienced a pilgrimage anywhere? Share that experience with other people in your group.
- How different is a pilgrimage from long-distance travel to another place?
- If your religion required you to devote three of weeks of life to a pilgrimage each year, would you sign up?

Crossing the frontiers and borders on the way

A cursory look at the political map – see Map 2.1 – soon makes you aware that for Jesus and his family, the pilgrimage to Jerusalem meant crossing between territories under different political rulers. Crossing the borders today in Palestine and Israel is an anxiety-causing experience. You encounter numerous sets of turnstiles, passport controls, metal detectors and intimidating armed soldiers. It is a brutal experience, sometimes exacerbated by the obvious pleasure that some operatives have at keeping people waiting or making life difficult – power in the hands of the small-minded. However, while experiences like this fuel the imagination, it is important that we do not impose the modern experience upon Jesus, his family and followers. So what was it like to cross the frontiers then?

While there may not have been passport control and turnstiles, crossing the various frontiers would have cost you in the ancient equivalent of the shekel as you paid the requisite toll prices. Here we should remember the follower of Jesus who had attended a tax booth at the border close to Capernaum: 'As he was walking along, he saw Levi son of Alphaeus sitting at the tax booth, and he said to him, "Follow me"' (Mark 2.14); 'As Jesus was walking along, he saw a man called Matthew sitting at the tax booth; and he said to him, "Follow me"' (Matt. 9.9).

Christopher Mann comments that 'this would be a tax-collection service for Herod Antipas, collecting taxes on goods passing through his territory from the neighbouring jurisdictions of Herod Philip and the Ten Towns'.[5] The animosity in the Gospels towards officials like Levi/Matthew makes us aware that getting past them was no small matter. So although the experience was perhaps not as intimidating as border crossing today, our pilgrims would still have felt that sense of powerlessness that can accompany being in the hands of a manipulative figure who had the power of the gate.

From Nazareth to Scythopolis

But the cost was more than financial. 'Galilee' is usually understood to be a shortened form of the Hebrew phrase *galil ha-goyim*, which means 'circle of the peoples'. And the Galilean Jewish community was indeed encircled by peoples from different ethnic and religious backgrounds. Within a short distance of home, Jesus and his family were in the foreign land, the land of the 'Greek' cities known as the Decapolis.

After crossing the border, the key city to circumnavigate would have been Scythopolis (modern Beth Shean), for they would surely have headed east once they left the Nazareth range of hills. Today the journey from Nazareth to Beth Shean is straightforward: you head down Route 60 from Nazareth to Afula, and then take Route 71 to Beth Shean. The distance is 37.2 km or 23.2 miles. I don't suppose it would have been much further on foot for Jesus. Close in geographical terms, in terms of culture, it was as far apart as Athens and Jerusalem!

The Greek name of Scythopolis probably derived from the settlement of a colony of Scythian veterans during the period when Israel was under the rule of the Ptolemies in the third century BCE. According to Herodotus, the Scythians were devotees of the wine god Dionysus.[6] And it is certain that the cult of Dionysus was alive and well in Scythopolis when the land came under Seleucid rule in the second century BCE, for the city acquired the name of Nysa under the Seleucid rulers. Nysa was the place in the myths to which Dionysus' nurse was banished and buried. Eric Meyers and Mark Chancey point out that the inhabitants refer to themselves in various inscriptions as 'Nysaean Scythopolis'.[7] In addition to being devotees of Dionysus, there was a high place near the city centre that most likely had a temple dedicated to Zeus.

In the period under Herodian and Roman rule, relations with Jewish neighbours seem to have been mainly peaceable. However, in the upheaval associated with the First Jewish War

(66–73 CE), a particularly tragic loss of life occurred at Scythopolis. Josephus relates that the 13,000 Jews who lived there
refused to join with their fellow Jews in the uprising against
Roman and Herodian rule. He wrote that their motives were
that they regarded 'their own security as more important than
the ties of blood'.[8] Despite this show of loyalty, he reported that
the Gentile citizens of Scythopolis massacred the lot!

Sean Freyne suggests that the peasants of Galilee most likely
visited Scythopolis for the purposes of trade and festivals. He
also thinks that the Dionysus cult was not a million miles away
from the Jewish faith, particularly at the time of the Feast of
Tabernacles, which celebrated the grape harvest.[9] I have my
doubts: for a Jewish family like that of Jesus, on their way to
the holy city of Jerusalem for the purposes of worship, how
would Scythopolis have seemed? What would they have made
of its theatres, pagan temples, unclean food and other Gentile
culture? Surely they would not have wanted to risk potential
defilement, and would have done their best to skirt around it,
keeping contact to a minimum.

Questions for reflection or discussion

I don't know if you have ever experienced culture shock, but
for me the most acute case I had of it was when we visited
my eldest son Joshua for the first time in Tokyo. Few people
spoke English and I could read hardly any of the writing on
public buildings. There was an abundance of beautiful, religious
architecture to be seen – particularly ornate Buddhist temples
and the iconic Torii gates to Shinto shrines – but a paucity of
familiar and comfortable symbols that an English Christian would
recognize. Joshua took us to visit local people, and we experienced the rituals of removing our shoes, sitting cross-legged
around a low table on titami (straw) mats and being served
green tea by a polite and gracious host. It tasted vile – at least

to my taste – but you could not let on, and you certainly could not let your smile drop. I began to be so anxious that I was not reading the cultural code that I became ill and succumbed to tonsillitis. I ended up spending time in bed (or rather in a duvet on the floor of a hotel room), while my wife, Wendy, Joshua and Isaac, my younger son, went out for the day without me. When I woke from sleep I discovered that I was still alone, so I popped out to a local store to buy some food. Purchasing what I thought was a jam doughnut, I returned to my room, relishing the prospect of some familiar pleasure. However, when I bit into the doughnut, to my horror the jam was curry paste. It was a cultural nightmare, but one that stretched me and made me much more aware of what it might be like for others to come to territory that for me is familiar and safe.

I am suggesting that Scythopolis would have caused Jesus and his family to have experienced culture shock.

- When and where have you experienced culture shock?
- What strategies did you adopt to cope with it?

From Scythopolis through Samaria

On leaving Scythopolis, Jesus' family had two options, as I explained earlier in this chapter. Either they could take the road to the south to Jerusalem via the Samaritan territory or they could head east across the Jordan via Pella, another of the cities of the Decapolis, into Perea, which was also under the rule of Antipas.

The Samaritan option was less distance and was clearly taken, both to and from Jerusalem, if the pilgrim was in a hurry (or tired), as the Gospels verify.

When the days drew near for him to be taken up, he set his face to go to Jerusalem. And he sent messengers ahead of him. On their way they entered a village of the Samaritans to make ready for him; but they did not receive him, because his face was set towards Jerusalem. When his disciples James and John saw it, they said, 'Lord, do you want us to command fire to come down from heaven and consume them?' But he turned and rebuked them.   (Luke 9.51–55)

On the way to Jerusalem, Jesus was going through the region between Samaria and Galilee.   (Luke 17.11)

[Jesus] left Judea and started back to Galilee. But he had to go through Samaria. So he came to a Samaritan city called Sychar, near the plot of ground that Jacob had given to his son Joseph. Jacob's well was there, and Jesus, tired out by his journey, was sitting by the well. It was about noon. A Samaritan woman came to draw water, and Jesus said to her, 'Give me a drink' . . . The Samaritan woman said to him, 'How is it that you, a Jew, ask a drink of me, a woman of Samaria?' (Jews do not share things in common with Samaritans.)   (John 4.3–9)

It is interesting that Jesus forbade his disciples to evangelize the Samaritans – 'Go nowhere among the Gentiles, and enter no town of the Samaritans, but go rather to the lost sheep of the house of Israel' (Matt. 10.5–6). Consequently many scholars regard the story in John 4 as a projection back to the time of Jesus of the later activity of early Christians, when some Samaritans had embraced the new movement (see Acts 8.5–25). In other words, it anticipates the Samaritan Christian mission and makes Jesus the pioneer himself.

Whatever we make of this debate, the snippets from the Gospels above make abundantly clear that Jewish pilgrims did pass through Samaritan terrain to and from Jerusalem. Equally, they illustrate the risks entailed in this journey and allude to the less than flattering antipathy felt on both sides of this religious divide.[10]

In the Jewish mind the Samaritans were religiously suspect. This is all the more surprising given that the Samaritan religion is closely related to the Jewish faith. The Samaritans, like the Jewish community, held the five books of the Law to be most sacred, as Reinhard Plummer has highlighted:

there was no iron curtain that went down between Jews and Samaritans, although on the whole each group embarked on a separate path. The Samaritans absolutized the Torah to such a degree that the Prophets and the Writings did not become part of their sacred scripture. Nor did they participate in the development of the *halakah* and *aggadah* contained in the Mishnah and Talmudim. Instead they developed their own legal and other traditions. But all important in Samaritanism remains the Torah.[11]

So they had much in common with their Jewish neighbours. However, they had different versions about the origin of the other:

> According to the Samaritans themselves, they are the original Israelites from whom the Jews split off in a schism under Eli who moved the ark of the covenant from Shechem to Shiloh . . . The traditional Jewish version sees the origins of the Samaritans in the events related in 2 Kings 17. This makes the Samaritans a mixture of pagans and inhabitants of the northern kingdom that had not been deported [by the Assyrians in the eighth century BCE].[12]

So in the minds of most Jews – even the more liberal – the Samaritans were really Gentiles in disguise. But at the heart of the dispute between the two religious communities lie the traditions surrounding David's election and the divine choice of Mount Zion as the locus of the Temple (see, for example, 2 Sam. 7.5–16; Ps. 132). In contradiction, the Samaritans held that Mount Gerizim was the mountain God chose for his Temple. It follows from the range of their Scriptures that with the Samaritans, there simply was room neither for King David nor Jerusalem in their theology – it was as if David had never happened.

The conflict between the Jewish and Samaritan communities was certainly exacerbated at the time of Jesus by recent history. The Samaritan Temple on Mount Gerizim had been destroyed by the Hasmonean ethnarch, high priest and prophet, John Hyrcanus (134–105 BCE). Hyrcanus was seeking by force of arms to create a Jewish state comprising both Jews and related ethnic groups in the vicinity. His conquest of Samaria and destruction of the Temple were all of a piece with his conservative religious outlook. Hyrcanus is also remembered for compelling the Idumeans or Edomites to undergo circumcision – one can only imagine the resentment harboured by these ethnic groups to this kind of zealotry.

So in the period with which we are concerned, the chasm was if anything wider than it had ever been. And we certainly get a flavour of the vitriolic nature of this dispute and the depth of antipathy between Jewish and Samaritan people in the story told in Luke 9 above, in which James and John requested permission from Jesus to call fire down upon the Samaritan village that refused them entry. Their response evokes the stories of Elijah (cf. 2 Kings 1), and enables us to understand why their nickname was Boanerges, 'Sons of Thunder' (Mark 3.17). Clearly sibling rivalry and internecine strife can be the most violent.

In the light of this atmosphere of animosity and mistrust, Galilean pilgrims would have been well advised to give the Samaritans a wide berth – better to plan for the long route by the Transjordan. Gerd Theissen and Annette Merz agree: 'a route through Peraea is more probable. That was the only way of avoiding setting foot on non-Jewish land'.[13]

Questions for reflection or discussion

- Are there any examples of strife between people or religious groups who hold very similar beliefs and shared values that have impacted upon your life and experience?
- Who might be for you the equivalent of the Samaritans?
- Are there people and communities you deliberately avoid?

3
Jesus: his journey (part 2)

From Scythopolis through Perea

If what I have said above about the dangers to a family group involved in traversing Samaritan territory is correct, then Jesus' family would have taken the long way. They would have crossed the Jordan near Scythopolis, skirted the city of Pella and entered Perea, the second territory under the Tetrarch Herod Antipas. Better the devil you know!

Perea is a name derived from the Greek adverb *peran*, meaning 'on the other side'. Josephus described it as follows:

> Perea, though far more extensive [than Galilee] is for the most part desert and rugged and too wild to bring tender fruits to maturity. However, there, too, are tracts of finer soil which are productive of every species of crop; and the plains are covered with a variety of trees, olive, vine, and palm being those principally cultivated. The country is watered by torrents descending from the mountains and by springs which never dry up.[1]

Josephus evidently focused on the positives about this landscape, because although it was a safe passage with a decent road, it was a dry and dusty route. And at one point you had to cross the difficult Wadi Jabbok. On foot you would need to be a determined traveller and well equipped with water containers.

At the end of your day of trudging in barren but breathtaking landscapes, the Jordan valley road would have brought you to the palm trees around the town of Betharamphtha, which was somewhere beyond the Jordan opposite the ancient city of Jericho.

Here Jesus' family would been confronted by one of the perplexing aspects of Herodian rule. The city of Betharamphtha, like Sepphoris, had also suffered from the outbreak of revolt after the death of Herod the Great in 4 BCE.[2] Antipas had restored the city. After completing the building works, he had renamed the city as Julias in honour of Livia, the wife of Augustus the Emperor.[3] This might sound innocuous, but it was much more than a honorific act.

The Herodian dynasty relied entirely upon the Emperor for their power. When Herod died it was Augustus who determined how his kingdom would be divided up. Get on the wrong side of him, and you could just as quickly lose your domain, as Antipas' older brother Archelaus would discover (see below). So the Herodian family walked a tightrope. On the one hand they wanted to appear to be faithful Jews ruling over Jews. This was most apparent in the decision by Herod, Archelaus and Antipas not to mint coins that bore their image so as not to offend Jewish sensitivities about representational art. It was also surely part of the reason why Herod invested so much of his energy and financial resources into transforming the Temple in Jerusalem into one of the wonders of the ancient world. But on the other hand the Herodians were also political realists who knew whence their power derived. At the same time as Herod was aggrandizing the Temple, he also embarked on another project on the coast at Strato's Tower. According to Josephus the work took twelve years.[4] At the end his engineers had constructed 'a citywide monument to imperial culture', named Caesarea Maritima or Caesarea by the Sea. Given pride of place in this new city, facing west to Rome, was an Augusteum, a temple dedicated to Augustus and the goddess Roma. Meyers and Chancey comment that 'it was apparently the first temple of the imperial cult in the Near East and one of the earliest anywhere in the empire'.[5]

Antipas was never in the same league as his father when it came to building projects. Even so he made an impact, as we noted in Chapter 1, with his rebuilding of Sepphoris and founding of Tiberias. And when it came to fealty to his Roman overlords, he was cut from the same cloth as his father. Once Betharamphtha had become Julias, we can have little doubt that it would have had an imperial temple to house a religious cult and a statue of Livia, something akin to what can be seen today in the Louvre in Paris.[6] Livia is unambiguously represented as a goddess figure. As the wife of a man who was regarded as the bringer of peace to the world, she is the mother of the Empire, and holds a cornucopia as symbol of the fruits of the earth – it does not take much imagination to see that a Jewish family on their way to Jerusalem would have found such propaganda deeply offensive. For them, the source of all the good things of the land lay in the gift of the Lord, the God of Israel. Julias would have confirmed for them that at the core of Antipas' reign lay the rot of unacceptable compromise.

Questions for reflection or discussion

- Are there ways in which we, like the Herodians, find ourselves walking a difficult tightrope?
- What are the powerful idols in our modern world that clamour for our attention and seek to compel us to offer compromising fealty?

Across the Jordan and into Judea

In nearing Jerusalem, Galilean pilgrims entered yet another political entity, the territory of Judea. When Herod died, Augustus made Archelaus, son of Herod and Malthace (born *c*.23 BCE), 'ethnarch' of Judea, Samaritis and Idumea. His domain included the important cities of Sebaste and Caesarea Maritima. Intriguingly, Augustus held back from giving him the title of king.

Within a decade Archelaus' subjects, both Jewish and Samaritan, tired of his harsh treatment and exploitation, and sent envoys to Augustus petitioning him for justice. Archelaus was subsequently deposed, exiled to Vienna and had his property confiscated.[7] This all took place around 5–6 CE.

Judea now came under the direct rule of the Romans through the governors who were based for most of the year in Caesarea Maritima. During the lifetime of Jesus, the Roman governors of Judea were as follows:

Coponius	*c.*6–9 CE
Marcus Ambivulus	*c.*9–12 CE
Annius Rufus	*c.*12–15 CE
Valerius Gratus	*c.*15–26 CE
Pontius Pilate	*c.*26–36 CE

These momentous changes were, as one may imagine, accompanied by significant political upheaval, which is aptly described by Lester Grabbe:

> Once Archelaus had been exiled in 6 C.E., it was necessary to set up the Roman administrative system in place of the Herodian one. This meant that taxation had to be done directly, rather than through the king or ethnarch . . . and to determine the tax liability of each person required an assessment of personal property. Hence the first task of Quirinius, the Syrian legate, and Coponius, the governor of Judea, was to consider a registration or census of persons and property. That this was an unprecedented action is quite clear because of the Jewish reaction. Many were very upset by it, although most acceded to the arguments of the high priest that there was nothing to do but submit. However, Judas the Galilean and Zaddok the Pharisee . . . led some sort of rebellion. Their view was that only God was their master and to accept the assessment was to submit to slavery.[8]

By the time Jesus was about 12 years old, things had settled down somewhat. But the memories of these turbulent times would not have been far from the surface.

Jericho was of course the gateway to Judea. The Galilean pilgrims' experience of crossing the Jordan and coming to Jericho must have been most welcome. Not only had they left behind 'idolatrous' Julias but they had come into territory more akin to home turf; that is, more recognizably Jewish in feel. This would have been enhanced by the significant change in landscape. Josephus provides the following description of the area:

> Jericho lies in a plain, but above it hangs a bare and barren mountain range of immense length, extending northwards as far as the territory of Scythopolis and southwards to the region of Sodom and the extremities of Lake Asphaltitis; this hill country is all rugged and owing to its sterility uninhabited.[9]

The barrenness of the landscape and the mountains around Jericho form such a stark contrast with this ancient city (see Plate 3.1). At one moment you are in something akin to a moonscape, then you are in a place where life is abundant, all made possible by the miracle of the springs that flow near Jericho, which never seem to dry up (see Plate 3.2 overleaf).

Plate 3.1 The verdant fields of Jericho stand out against the backdrop of the barren mountains
Source Photograph by the author.

Plate 3.2 Elishah's Spring, near Jericho – water bringing life in a barren place
Source Photograph courtesy of Todd Bolen/BiblePlaces.com.

In our part of the world, a drop of rain is usually interpreted as something negative or unpleasant. Here, you might like to listen to Queen's famous song, 'Rain must fall', from their 1989 album, *The Miracle.* The lyrics, sung so hauntingly by Freddie Mercury, contrast days full of sunshine with the hard realities, symbolized by 'rain', that can catch up with us from time to time. Quite understandable in the UK, where even in May cold rain can fall on your face when you are hoping for a warm spring day! In sharp distinction from this perspective, after the parched land-scape of Perea you would have been desperate for a little rain to fall upon you. How welcome must have been the sight of a drop of water in Jericho – heavenly in fact.

Jericho was yet another border city, so yet another palm must be crossed with shekels. It is noteworthy, therefore, that Luke recounts that Jericho was the home of the notorious tax collector, Zacchaeus (Luke 19.1–11). Jesus' radical hospitality to this man, who was shunned for understandable reasons, brought about a transformation in this man's life every bit as miraculous as the miracle of the city itself.

At this point in the journey Jesus and his family may have felt that the end was in view – just over one day's walk ahead and then it's the outskirts of Jerusalem. However, that would be a mistaken perspective. The road from here was notorious. On the one hand there was the serious geographical challenge: parallel to the Wadi Kelt, the road rises 1,000 metres (3,250 feet) in 22–23 km (about 14 miles). But the road was also a hotbed for brigands and opportunists who took advantage both of the nooks and crannies in which to hide and of the pilgrims and traders on their way to the great city for the festivals. That is why Jesus' story about the traveller who was attacked on the Jericho road struck such a chord: 'A man was going down from Jerusalem to Jericho, and fell into the hands of robbers, who stripped him, beat him, and went away, leaving him half dead' (Luke 10.30–35). I suspect that Jesus and his family may well have helped such strangers on this road.

This real and present danger posed by the pilgrimage is something that Sean Freyne highlights: 'Galileans encountered dangers in making the pilgrimage to Jerusalem, not just those inherent in travel in antiquity generally.'[10] It might also explain the cryptic words Jesus speaks to the disciples at the Last Supper:

> He said to them, 'When I sent you out without a purse, bag, or sandals, did you lack anything?' They said, 'No, not a thing.' He said to them, 'But now, the one who has a purse must take it, and likewise a bag. And the one who has no sword must sell his cloak and buy one. For I tell you, this scripture must be fulfilled in me, "And he was counted among the lawless"; and indeed what is written about me is being fulfilled.' They said, 'Lord, look, here are two swords.' He replied, 'It is enough.'
>
> (Luke 22.35–38)

I have often wondered how they were able to find a couple of swords at such short notice. Perhaps fear evoked by the Jericho

road led some of his followers not to take his advice to travel
so lightly!

Questions for reflection or discussion

- What or where have you found oases or sources of refresh-
  ment in your journey of faith?
- To what extent do you feel that you face real and present
  danger as you try to travel faithfully with Jesus today?
- Who have been the people who were like the Good Samaritan
  who picked up you up when you had been knocked about?
- Is there anyone that you know who has been waylaid that
  you could help back on the journey of faith?

4

Jerusalem, journey's end

I grew up in Lincolnshire in a village called Hibaldstow, in the northern part of the county. It is a little more than 48 km (20 miles) north of Lincoln, and was then on the main road, the A15, which followed the route of the ancient Roman road known as Ermine Street. Possibly once or twice each summer my parents used to take us along the road to Lincoln to visit an aunt who lived beyond Lincoln in Newark.

Once we got onto Ermine Street proper, just after the tiny hamlet of Redbourne, I used to marvel at how straight the road was, stretching out in the distance, visible for miles because of the relatively flat landscape. I allowed my imagination to flit back 1,800 years or so and visualized cohorts of Roman foot soldiers running in formation along this road, perhaps accompanied by the eagle standard. What a sight they must have made! But the magic of this great road grew after the car passed Caenby Corner, for looming out of the mists, with miles still to cover, appeared the unmistakable outline of Lincoln Cathedral. The journey still held the excitement of passing RAF Scampton, with its security fencing and Wellington bomber out front, and the evocation of those myth-like pilot heroes of the Second World War, such as Douglas Bader. But the heart was still gripped by the presence of that silhouette of the cathedral, inviting you to keep going onwards, and to ignore the distractions of the way. Sometimes our return journey was in the dark. From the Newark side the cathedral was just as impressive, especially because it was lit up with mighty beams of light that made it stand out in the night sky.

This was my first experience of pilgrimage and the magnetism of sacred space. These childhood experiences also helped me to identify with Jesus' words:

> You are the light of the world. A city built on a hill cannot be hidden. No one after lighting a lamp puts it under the bushel basket, but on the lampstand, and it gives light to all in the house. In the same way, let your light shine before others, so that they may see your good works and give glory to your Father in heaven. (Matt. 5.14–16)

I imagined that Jesus had been inspired by the twinkling of lights of Jerusalem as he sat on the Mount of Olives. Whether or not this speculation is correct, Jerusalem cuts a fine vista today as you approach it from the summit of the Mount of Olives either by day or night (see Plate 4.1).

Obviously, the view is now dominated by the great Dome of the Rock Mosque, which sits on the massive platform built for the Temple by Herod the Great. It is truly a breathtaking panorama, and if we could strip away the modern buildings we would get an even greater sense of the scale of the Temple

Plate 4.1 Jerusalem from the Mount of Olives
Source Photograph by the author.

Plaza and the city as a whole. To help us do that we cannot do much better than ponder the painting by the Victorian artist Edward Lear, *Jerusalem from the Mount of Olives, Sunrise.*[1] Lear's painting of 1859 most certainly accentuates the way the ancient city would have stood out from its surrounding landscape. He gives us a real feel for what Jesus' family would have experienced as they came over the brow of the hill from Bethphage and gazed towards the city with its great Temple.

Questions for reflection or discussion

- What places have caused your heart to skip a beat as you approached them?
- How have journeys to settings like these changed the way you viewed your normal life?

Casing the joint

Having begun to consider the impact of the city of Jerusalem upon a young man from tiny Nazareth in Galilee, let's take in some of the sights, with the pilgrims.

I would imagine that a young lad from Nazareth would want to walk the walls of the city soon after arriving. No better way to get a sense of the city's layout (see Map 4.1 overleaf).

The city was fortified by three walls, except where it was enclosed by impassable ravines, a single rampart there sufficing. It was built, in portions facing each other, on two hills separated by a central valley, in which tiers of houses ended. Of these hills that on which the upper city lay was far higher and had a straighter ridge than the other; consequently, owing to its strength it was called by King David . . . the Stronghold, but we called it the upper agora [market]. The second hill, which bore the name of Acra and supported the lower city, was a hog's back. Opposite this was a third hill, by nature lower than Acra, and once

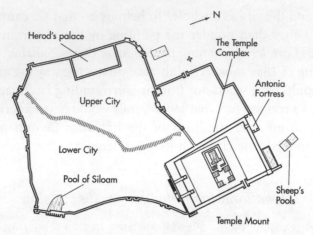

Map 4.1 Jerusalem in the time of Jesus

Source David Wenham and Steve Walton, *Exploring the New Testament*, vol. 1, *The Gospels and Acts*, 2nd edn (London: SPCK, 2011), p. 21.

divided from it by another broad ravine. Afterwards, however, the Hasmoneans, during the period of their reign, both filled up the ravine, with the object of uniting the city to the temple, and also reduced the elevation of the Acra by levelling its summit, in order that it might not block the view of the temple.[2]

After wandering the walls, you would no doubt want to go close to the Temple without actually going up – save that for the day of the sacrifice. As you did so, another sight that would have grabbed the eye would have been the great stones of the Temple foundations (see Plate 4.2) – 'As he came out of the temple, one of his disciples said to him, "Look, Teacher, what large stones and what large buildings!"' (Mark 13.1).

It is really hard to convey the scale of the ashlars in the south-west corner of the Temple Mount and the Temple complex itself. Some of them are 10 metres (32 feet) in length and weigh about 50 tons. They supported a sacred precinct of gigantic proportions. It was 480 metres (1,575 feet) long by 280 metres (920 feet) wide.[3] That makes the circumference about 1.5 km (1 mile). To give you a sense of perspective from a British standpoint,

Plate 4.2 The foundation stones of the Temple Plaza
Source Photograph by the author.

the Temple plaza would be significantly larger than the new Wembley Stadium in London, which is 1 km in circumference.

Josephus, the first-century historian, could not be more expansive about the aesthetic impact of the Temple building itself:

> The exterior of the building wanted nothing that could astound either mind or eye. For, being covered on all sides with massive plates of gold, the sun was no sooner up than it radiated so fiery a flash that persons straining to look at it were compelled to avert their eyes, as from the solar rays. To approaching strangers it appeared from a distance like a snow-clad mountain; for all that was not overlaid with gold was of purest white. From its summit protruded sharp golden spikes to prevent birds from settling upon and polluting the roof.[4]

Exaggeration? Yes. Even so, it must have been an awe-inspiring sight (see Figure 4.1 overleaf). But even here in the heartland of the Jewish community, ambiguity was present, as Eric Myers and Mark Chancey have pointed out:

> Herod's rebuilt Temple complex exhibited a combination of Jewish, Near Eastern, Hellenistic, and Roman influences. The

Figure 4.1 Reconstruction drawing of the Temple Mount by Leen Ritmeyer

Source Leen Ritmeyer, *The Quest: Revealing the Temple Mount in Jerusalem* (Jerusalem: Carta, 2006), p. 19. Used with permission.

spatial organisation of the naos [the holiest part of the Temple] reflected priestly descriptions of the Tabernacle (Exod 25—30, 35—39). The placement of a sanctuary within a temenos [what I have called the 'plaza'] was typical of temples in the Hellenized East, though not the Roman West, but the sheer size of the Herodian temenos separated it from contemporary examples. The massive complex was the largest in the Roman Empire and one of the biggest anywhere in the Roman world. Its extensive use of columns reflected a Roman appropriation of an earlier Hellenistic architectural motif, with distinctively Roman influence most strikingly apparent in the basilical shape of the Royal Portico. Thus, while the newly renovated Temple remained an expression of local Jewish culture, it also brought Rome right to the centre of Jerusalem. The most sacred site in Judaism was now decorated with Roman architecture.[5]

Question for reflection or discussion

- What are the places or institutions that you admire, but also disturb you because they bring together things you feel should be kept apart?

Negotiating the crowds

Herod's enhanced or supercharged Temple was indeed ambiguous, but you cannot doubt the business plan of Herod the Great. This was a centre designed for throngs of people, both from the land itself and also from the Jewish diaspora. The crowds converging on the city must have been amazing, but also disconcerting. Josephus makes a wild guess at the numbers:

> on the occasion of the feast called the Passover, at which they sacrifice from the ninth to the eleventh hour, and a little fraternity, as it were, gathers round each sacrifice, of not fewer than ten persons . . . while the companies often include as many as twenty, the victims were counted and amounted to two hundred and fifty-five thousand six hundred; allowing an average of ten diners to each victim, we obtain a total of two million seven hundred thousand, all pure and holy.[6]

His arithmetic was not very good, was it! Josephus notes that this figure excluded people afflicted with ritual defilements and foreigners. Thus elsewhere he goes for a round figure of three million.[7] Anyone who has been in a large crowd can well appreciate how hard it is to be accurate about the numbers involved. For example, I took part in the 2011 Palm Sunday procession from Bethphage to St Stephen's Gate (see Plate 4.3 overleaf). In the claustrophobic press of people I have no idea how many were there – I would guess around 10,000, but it would be easy to exaggerate upwards.

Hard-headed scholars like Joachim Jeremias have pruned down Josephus' number of Passover lambs to 18,000, and suggested that the number of 180,000 – including about 55,000 inhabitants of Jerusalem – is closer to the reality.[8] E. P. Sanders, on the other hand, is willing to countenance from 300,000 to 500,000 people. He links this to Tacitus' report that the besieged city of Jerusalem in 70 CE held 600,000 people,[9] and also makes comparisons with pre-Second World

Plate 4.3 Palm Sunday pilgrims walking down the Mount of Olives (2011)
Source Photograph by the author.

War numbers of pilgrims at Mecca. These exceeded 100,000, and Mecca was a more difficult location to get to than ancient Jerusalem.[10]

So not three million – but 300,000–500,000 pilgrims are still amazing numbers, and you wonder where they all stayed! And yet according to the Mishnah, no one was heard to say, 'The crowd is too great, I cannot find shelter in Jerusalem.'[11]

Here another aspect of this experience needs to be mentioned, namely the multi-ethnic identity of the Jewish pilgrims visiting Jerusalem for the festival. Acts 2.7–11 gives a list of these Jewish groups:

Amazed and astonished, they asked, 'Are not all these who are speaking Galileans? And how is it that we hear, each of us, in our own native language? Parthians, Medes, Elamites, and residents of Mesopotamia, Judea and Cappadocia, Pontus and Asia, Phrygia and Pamphylia, Egypt and the parts of Libya belonging to Cyrene, and visitors from Rome, both Jews and proselytes, Cretans and Arabs – in our own languages we hear them speaking about God's deeds of power.'

Perhaps this is a somewhat stylized list, but it surely reflects the reality that 'travel from abroad to Jerusalem took place from the whole of the known world, mainly from "Syria, Babylonia, Egypt and Asia Minor"'.[12] Whatever Herod may have had in mind when he set about enhancing the Temple site, and in building his new port at Caesarea Maritima, this was surely part of the grand plan.

Questions for reflection or discussion

- Imagine the impact upon a young boy from wee small Nazareth of encountering these huge crowds and this kaleidoscopic, cosmopolitan collection of Jews.
- What experiences do you have of being in large crowds of people?
- What range of feelings did this evoke in you?

Taking in the stately homes, from afar

The city was divided into two parts – the upper city in the west and the lower city in the east. In the upper city were the homes of the spectacularly rich. These were clustered around Herod's vast palace, with its, 'two large wings, raised on a podium to create a platform for the requisite structures, gardens and pools, and overlooked by three great towers'.[13] This was somewhere near the modern Jaffa Gate. Herod called the towers Hippicus, after his friend, Phasaelis, after his brother and Mariamme, after his wife.[14] Parts of them still survive. Again we turn to Josephus for a description of the splendour of Herod's palace:

> the king's palace, baffling all description: indeed, in extravagance and equipment no building surpassed it. It was completely enclosed within a wall thirty cubits high, broken at equal distances by ornamental towers, and contained immense banqueting-halls and bed-chambers for one hundred guests. The interior fittings

are indescribable – the variety of the stones . . . ceilings wonderful both for the length of the beams and the splendour of their surface decoration, the host of apartments with their infinite varieties of design, all amply furnished, while most of the objects in each of them were of silver or gold. All around were many circular cloisters, leading one into another, the columns in each being different, and their open courts all of greensward; there were groves of various trees intersected by long walks, which were bordered by deep canals, and ponds everywhere studded with bronze figures, through which the water was discharged, and around the streams were numerous cots for tame pigeons.[15]

Perhaps a degree of poetic licence was taken here to highlight what was lost in the later tragedy of the destruction of the city. However, as Josephus also pointed out, the palace was not destroyed by the Romans but by 'the ravages of the brigands' fire' at the beginning of the revolt.[16] Unfortunately, he does not ask why they should have done this. The implication is that there was some resentment from the brigands towards the Jewish aristocracy and rulers. And it is plain there was some kind of social distance between upper city and lower city Jerusalem. It was in the lower city that those who belonged to the despised professions would be found living and plying their trades. The weavers were in the despised neighbourhood outside the Dung Gate.[17] The leather industry was required to be set up in the east side of town; that is, in the lower city, at least 50 cubits – about 23 metres (25 yards) – distant.[18] The Mishnah explicitly states that this was related to the aromas surrounding this trade. By contrast, luxury items such as ointments and resins had trading centres in the upper city.[19]

The opulence of Herod's palace was not exactly matched by the homes of the aristocratic priestly families in the upper city. However, they were clearly in keeping with the setting, as confirmed by the archaeological work by Nahman Avigad in the Jewish quarter of the old city after the 1967 war (now on display in the Wohl Archaeological Museum). Whether the pilgrims from Nazareth ever got to see the inside of one of these palatial stately homes is debatable. Jeremias suggests that 'there is reliable evidence that at Passover time in Jerusalem poor people were invited in from the street'.[20] However, I would imagine that family groups like those from Nazareth were unlikely to fit into this category. What is not in dispute is the huge gulf between these mansions and the simple homes of Nazareth.

'Come and spend your tithe in Jerusalem!'

No visit to modern Jerusalem is complete without the mandatory visit to the souvenir shops, and it cannot have been much different then. Indeed, it would seem that this was built into the Torah. Deuteronomy required that people consumed a tithe of their income in Jerusalem itself, every year except the seventh, which was meant to be a fallow year (Deut. 14.22–26). In the third year it was to be given to the Levite, the poorer assistants of the Temple priests, and the needy. This legislation sounds like an ingenious way to ensure that people saved up for their holidays and also supported Jerusalem financially.[21] No doubt the local shopkeepers rubbed their hands with glee as the Passover season approached, much like high street shop proprietors do today as December looms.

There would have been markets in both halves of the city. Jeremias refers to a form of souvenir shopping that would have appealed to the elite:

> Frequent mention is made of a piece of jewellery called . . . 'the golden city' . . . This ornament is also called 'golden Jerusalem' . . . In the *Aboth de Rabbi Nathan* 6a and elsewhere, it is said that only ladies of high rank wore this jewel. So 'the golden Jerusalem' was a costly ornament for women. It may be imagined as a kind of *corona muralis*, and the name . . . suggests that the ornament was originally made in Jerusalem . . . we may well conclude that such items of jewellery were widely bought as souvenirs there.[22]

This tiara sounds like a form of enterprise culture – long before the Beefeater hats of London! So much for the elite, but what was there for the hoi polloi? There seem to have been plenty of options. Jeremias finds evidence in various rabbinical sources for 'craftsmen' sitting at work in their shops open to the street, for shops in the Temple Court and on the Mount of Olives, for tailors positioning themselves near the gates of the city, bazaars of wool carders and merchants.[23] I imagine that pottery would be available bearing images of the furniture in the Temple such as the menorah (the seven-branched candelabra), miniature incense shovels, garments and items of clothing and festival-related treats or sweets.

Questions for reflection or discussion

- Do you practise the discipline of tithing?
- When you do, do you only imagine that it should be given to the Church for the work of ministry?
- How do you respond to the idea that a tithe can also be set aside for the purpose of family holidays?
- And when you plan your holidays, do you ever think how you might use them to ensure that the resources you spend bring life and employment to others, especially the poor of the world?

Preparing for the encounter with holiness

No visit to the Temple was possible without careful attention to ritual purity and what some have called 'graded holiness'. The following passage from the Mishnah gives us a vivid sense of the various levels of holiness associated with the Land, Jerusalem and the Temple:

> There are ten degrees of holiness. The Land of Israel is holier than any other land . . . The walled cities [of the land of Israel]

are still more holy, in that they must send forth the lepers from their midst; moreover they may carry a corpse therein wherever they will, but once it has gone forth [from the city] they may not bring it back.

Within the wall [of Jerusalem] is still more holy, for there [only] they may eat the Lesser Holy Things and the Second Tithe. The Temple Mount is still more holy, for no man or woman that has a flux, no menstruant, and no woman after childbirth may enter therein. The Rampart is still more holy, for no Gentiles and none that have contracted uncleanness from a corpse may enter therein. The Court of Women is still more holy, for none that had immersed himself the selfsame day [because of uncleanness] may enter therein, yet none would thereby become liable to a Sin-Offering. The Court of the Israelites is still more holy, for none whose atonement is yet incomplete may enter therein, and they would become liable to a Sin-Offering. The Court of Priests is still more holy, for Israelites may not enter therein save only when they must perform the laying on of hands, slaughtering and waving.

Between the Porch and the Altar is still more holy, for none that has a blemish or whose hair is unloosed may enter there. The Sanctuary is still more holy, for none may enter therein with hands and feet unwashed. The Holy of Holies is still more holy, for none may enter therein save only the High Priest on the Day of Atonement at the time of the [Temple] service.[24]

For Jesus and his family, visiting the Temple would certainly have brought them face to face with greater expectations about ritual purity than would have been a normal part of life in Nazareth. They could expect to be challenged as they approached the sacred precincts of the Temple by a priest or Levite calling out words like the following gate liturgy from the psalms:

> Who shall ascend the hill of the Lord?
>   And who shall stand in his holy place?
> Those who have clean hands and pure hearts,
>   who do not lift up their souls to what is false,
>   and do not swear deceitfully

They will receive blessing from the LORD,
and vindication from the God of their salvation
Such is the company of those who seek him,
who seek the face of the God of Jacob.

(Psalm 24.3–6)

They would also have been aware that there were dire consequences for those who ignored these expectations, as was confirmed by the sign discovered in 1871 by Charles Clermont-Ganneau: 'Let no Gentile enter within the partition and barrier surrounding the temple; whosoever is caught shall be responsible for his subsequent death.'[25] Presumably there were similar signs at each stage of the journey from the perimeter of the Temple precincts to its sacred centre.

Back in Galilee, wealthier people had access to private ritual baths or *miqveh*. This most likely reflected a laudable desire on their part to 'sacralize' life at home. However, this pattern of spiritual life would have been a luxury the general public could not afford. It is also improbable in this period that communal ritual baths existed in tiny villages like Nazareth. So the

Plate 4.4 A *miqveh* excavated on the west of the Temple Mount close to the piers for Robinson's Arch

Source Photograph by the author.

visit to the Temple entailed a whole new dimension of religious experience: that of total immersion in the cold waters of a *miqveh* (see Plate 4.4).

A fascinating papyrus fragment found in the dump in Oxyrhynchus in Egypt recounts a story about Jesus that is not known in the canonical Gospels but does help us understand the significance of ritual washing at the Temple:

> And taking along the disciples he entered the holy court and was walking about the Temple. And approaching, a certain Pharisee, a ruling priest, whose name was Levi met them and said to the Saviour, 'Who permitted you to walk in this place of purification and to see these holy vessels, when you have not washed nor yet have your disciples bathed their feet? But defiled you have walked in this Temple, which is a pure place, in which no other person walks unless he has washed himself and changed his clothes, neither does he dare view these holy vessels.' And the Saviour immediately stood [still] with his disciples and answered him, 'Are you then, being here in the Temple clean?' He says to him, 'I am clean, for I washed in the pool of David, and having descended by one set of steps I ascended by another. And I put on white and clean clothes, and then I came and looked upon these holy vessels.' Answering the Saviour said to him, 'Woe you blind who do not see. You have washed in these running waters in which dogs and swine have been cast night and day, and have cleaned and wiped the outside skin, which also harlots and flute-girls anoint and wash and wipe and beautify for the lust of men; but within they are full of scorpions and all wickedness. But I and my disciples, who you say have not bathed, have been dipped in the waters of eternal life which come from . . . But woe to the . . .[26]

The story contains some jarring elements that do not quite fit with Jerusalem of the first century – such as the reference to dogs and swine, unless these are meant to be read symbolically and pejoratively as an ironic reference to the 'clean', who are really the 'unclean' in disguise. It is also doubtful whether Jesus was ever quite as condemnatory of the ritual washing as this (see, for example, John 13.10). That said, the story certainly helps us make sense of the dividers that can be seen in the steps of some of the pools and also takes us into the world that the young Jesus would have encountered at the Temple.

Ritual washing was performed on the eve of your visit, in the nude – so segregation of the sexes would have been practised – and in the dark, so that the water might not become a breeding ground for mosquitoes! Descending into the dark, cold water in the early spring must have been a memorable experience. Perhaps those emerging from the waters would have felt exhilarated, almost like becoming a reborn human being. Given the Passover connections, they may also have identified themselves with the generation that passed through the Red Sea on their journey to the Land.[27]

Questions for reflection or discussion

- In some Christian traditions, baptismal vows are renewed by the sprinkling of water on Easter Sunday. Do you practise this discipline? How important is this for you?
- Could such a ritual help you to connect more deeply with the Passover faith of Jesus and Israel?

Ascending to the high and holy place

Having bathed the day before, Jesus and his family would have been ready to ascend the stairs to the Temple on Passover eve. Some of the ancient steps are still visible today, and their varying depth is striking – you get the impression this was deliberate and designed to prevent people from running up them and approaching holiness in a hurry.

The Temple was not just a remarkable place, it was also a complex institution: both a bank and a sanctuary. Here the

Temple officials brought the Temple tax, which is referred to in Matthew 17.24–27. This was gathered from the regions and levied from every Jewish male, both those in the Land and in the Diaspora. They paid with the Tyrian half-shekel, which controversially bore the image of an eagle.[28] It was used to support the continuous sacrifices offered day in day out at the Temple. The latter was not a small matter either – Hanson and Oakman calculate that every year 1,200 animals – bulls, oxen, rams and lambs – were needed.[29] So significant amounts of money were stored somewhere in the Temple. From time to time desperate Roman governors like Pilate and Florus could not refrain from raiding the vaults for money.[30]

In addition to handling the Temple tax, facilities must have been made available to handle the gifts and tithes that the people brought – there must have been financial officials who recorded these. Others would have handled the exchange of money – Roman money could not be used as it was defaced with the image of Caesar. Others would have inspected the animals brought for sacrifice to make sure they met the standards required by levitical law. Given that many pilgrims came from a distance, still other officials would have been selling the lambs required for the Passover sacrifice. The scale of the operation is mind-blowing: if 20 priests were needed each day for the daily sacrifices, what level of personnel was required when around 30,000–50,000 lambs needed to be sacrificed on the afternoon of Passover eve? Josephus may not be exaggerating when he says that as many as 1,500 priests were needed for the weekly services.[31]

The Court of the Gentiles, which was the outer court, had an area of about 35 acres. At Passover time it must have been more akin to a cattle and sheep market – just imagine the bleating, haggling, straw and manure that would greet you as you ascended the final stairwell from the Huldah gates.

Once they had paid their dues and bought their lamb, Jesus and his family could begin to go deeper into the Temple, leaving behind the noisy outer court. The next courtyard was called the Court of Women. At another gate, replete with warning sign and staff, Jesus and Joseph would have had to leave Mary behind. While she waited and prayed with the other female members of the family, they crossed the Court of Israel with their lamb and approached the gate of the Court of Priests. Here they would have queued and waited their turn as a squadron of priests went about their business of receiving one lamb after another. Perhaps they caught a glimpse of the smoking, blood-soaked bronze altar in the Court of Priests in front of the golden doors of the most sacred parts of the Temple. We have a tantalising description of what it was like to stand where Jesus and Joseph did in the *Letter of Aristeas*, a source from the second century BCE:

> The ministering of the priests was absolutely unsurpassable in its vigour and the arrangement of its well-ordered silence: All work hard of their own accord, with much exertion, and each one looks after his appointed task. Their service is unremitting, sharing the sacrifices, some undertaking the carrying of wood, others oil, others wheaten flour, others the sweet spices, others offering burnt offerings of the parts of the flesh – all of them exerting their strength in different ways ... A general silence reigns, so that one might think that there was not a single man in the place although the number of ministers in attendance is more than seven hundred, in addition to a large number of the assistants bringing forwards the animals for sacrifice.[32]

The Bronze Altar and the Court of Priests would have been awash with blood, something most of our modern and artistic representations tend to ignore. But the truth is that the Temple was more like a combination of a cathedral and slaughterhouse![33] A priest with blood-spattered garments would have returned a little later to Jesus and Joseph, bringing them their portions of the Passover lamb to be taken away and prepared for the festal meal later.[34]

A city with underlying tensions

That evening the family would have eaten their Passover meal in their lodgings. They would no doubt be full of joy and thankfulness for God's saving acts in the past and probably had hopeful expectations for the future. But as they ate, they would have been much aware that all was not well with the city and the nation. For one thing the nation was hardly united. As people from a rustic place like Nazareth they would surely have encountered the kind of prejudice that was born of the first-century north–south divide, which is noted in the fourth Gospel:

> 'Surely the Messiah does not come from Galilee, does he?' . . . 'But this crowd, which does not know the law – they are accursed.' . . . 'Surely you are not also from Galilee, are you? Search and you will see that no prophet is to arise from Galilee.'
>
> (John 7.41, 49, 51)

Some would argue that this is a slanted perspective of this Gospel, but it chimes in with the well-known saying later attributed to Johanan ben Zakkai: 'Galilee, Galilee, you hate the Torah!'[35]

Was this a case of regional snobbery and prejudice? Or was it, as Theissen and Merz suggest, reflective of a city/rural divide?[36] Either way it was hardly a fair assessment of such Jews who had faithfully come to Jerusalem on pilgrimage at great risk and cost to themselves – see further Josephus' portrayal of the Galileans as faithful Jews and Freyne's judicious comments.[37]

In addition to the sense that the people were not completely united, the other disturbing element was the presence of those watchful Gentile observers, who although trying to stay out of the way would nonetheless be noticed. By the time Jesus was about ten years old, the pilgrimage would have brought him and his family face to face with the reality that Judea was under direct Roman rule. The bare facts of the situation are summed up by Jeremias:

> After AD 6 Judaea was a Roman province with a Roman gover-
> nor, Roman troops and Roman officials. Jerusalem had a Roman
> garrison, namely a *cohors miliaria equitata* under a tribune, which
> would ensure frequent contact with Rome . . . in the garrison
> at Jerusalem, as was proper for a procuratorial province, even
> the officers were not Roman (Acts 22.28); but in Caesarea, the
> procurator's residence, was the so-called 'Italian Cohort' (Acts
> 10.1), and these troops no doubt were part of the procurator's
> escort on his customary appearance in Jerusalem at passover
> time.[38]

So how did Jerusalem appear to Jesus and his family when they arrived for the annual festival? Did it feel like an occupied city, akin to Paris during the Second World War? Or was it less 'in your face' than that?

The Passover was a particularly sensitive time for the Roman overlords. 'The feast embodied the theme of national libera-tion', and as such 'it was sometimes an occasion when unrest at Israel's current state led to riot'.[39] In 4 BCE, at the Passover some worshippers took the opportunity to protest against the execution of the two teachers who had inspired their students to remove the eagle over the entrance to the Temple. Archelaus the ethnarch deployed a cohort of troops to arrest the ring-leader. In the mayhem that followed, Josephus reported that 3,000 worshippers were killed, the remainder dispersed and the sacrifices cancelled.[40] Later, in 48–52 CE, during the pro-curatorship of Cumanus, another riot followed the provocative behaviour of a Roman soldier, standing guard on the roof of the portico of the Temple. Josephus wrote:

> a body of men in arms invariably mounts guard at the feasts,
> to prevent disorders arising from such a concourse of people.
> Thereupon, one of the soldiers, raising his robe, stooped in an
> indecent attitude, so as to turn his backside to the Jews, and
> made a noise in keeping with his posture.[41]

Plate 4.5 The Israeli Defence Force staff a watchtower near Herodium

Source Photograph by the author.

In the riot that followed, thousands died – 30,000 or 20,000 according to which Josephus source is consulted.[42]

How should we interpret these accounts? Were they exceptional disasters that formed a stark contrast with the normally quiet reality, or were they the outcome of resentment that festered year on year and boiled over on these two occasions because of ham-fisted management of the crowds? I rather suspect the latter is the case.

So the Jewish nation was being watched (and it would have known that it was), especially during the Passover, from the fortress known as Antonia. According to Josephus this building dominated the Temple in much the same way that the Temple dominated the city.[43] It is hard to imagine that the presence of the permanent garrison and the extras who came down from Caesarea Maritima were not noticed and even more that they were not resented (see Plate 4.5).

Questions for reflection or discussion

We have now completed our journey with Jesus from Nazareth to Jerusalem.

- What stands out for you as you reflect upon the fractured complex world of Jesus?
- Earlier we considered the contribution that a small place like Nazareth made during Jesus' formative years. How do you think an annual journey like this would have broadened his horizons?
- In your own experience, what has stretched your perspectives and given you a bigger picture?
- In your life, what are the sources of irritation and frustration? Who are the equivalent of the Jerusalem elites who do not value you and the Roman soldiers who watch you?
- Or perhaps you belong to those who have power and influence. Do you ever consider how others view you?

5

Jesus: his challenge

Introduction

Jesus' world was, as we have seen, complex and far from united
and harmonious. Regional, social, religious and racial divisions
were present in abundance. We turn now to consider how Jesus
brought a distinctive and challenging message to this world,
best summed up in the sayings preserved for us in the Sermon
on the Mount exhorting his followers to love their enemies,
pray for them and bless them. In this chapter I want to ask,
first, 'How distinctive was this call?' I will then consider some
responses to this radical teaching from leading thinkers of
various faiths and backgrounds.

Jesus' challenge

The key text is the following passage from the Sermon on the
Mount:

> You have heard that it was said, 'You shall love your neighbour
> and hate your enemy.' But I say to you, Love your enemies and
> pray for those who persecute you, so that you may be children
> of your Father in heaven; for he makes his sun rise on the evil
> and on the good, and sends rain on the righteous and on the
> unrighteous. (Matt. 5.43–45)

As long ago as the 1860s, the sceptical historian David
Strauss noted that here if anywhere we can hear the authentic
voice of Jesus Christ: 'If there is a speech in the New Testament
that came from the lips of Jesus, this certainly did so, and

Plate 5.1 A rhinoceros evocatively breaks through the modern Wall of Bethlehem – is this a good symbol for Jesus?
Source Photograph by the author.

was not put into his mouth at a later period.'[1] Strauss thought that this teaching was so unique that it can only have come from Jesus. Surely no Jewish or Christian author would have said anything quite as radical as this (see Plate 5.1).

Recently this line has been challenged. For example, the Jewish scholar David Flusser has argued that Jesus' teaching is continuous with the emerging ethics of the Jewish sages of that period. While Jesus did launch an assault on contemporary interpretations of obedience to the Torah, for Flusser this 'stemmed from attitudes already established before his time'.[2]

To understand the background to Flusser's perspective we need to be aware of the enormous impact of the life and military career of Alexander the Great. After his victories the world of Jewish communities in Israel was thrown upside down. The cultures of the east met an aggressive version of western Hellenistic culture, and the aftershocks were felt for centuries. Flusser's view is that in the context of an all-pervasive and powerful Hellenism, older tidy boundaries between Jew and Greek and between faithful and unfaithful Jew became harder to maintain. Such was the social and political upheaval that it became more difficult to divide rigidly and sharply between 'the righteous and sinners', and almost impossible to love only those who are good and to hate the wicked.

Flusser finds that what Luke presents Jesus as saying – 'Be merciful, just as your Father is merciful' (Luke 6.36) – was widely expressed. The Matthean parallel is, 'Be perfect, therefore, as your heavenly Father is perfect' (Matt. 5.48). Flusser approves the NEB translation: 'There must be no limits to your goodness, as your heavenly father's goodness knows no bounds.' He notes that here Jesus is close to the humane attitude of later Jewish rabbis like Abbahu (*c.*300 CE), who is cited in the Babylonian Talmud: 'The day when rain fails is greater than [the day of] the Revival of the Dead, for the Revival of the Dead is for the righteous only whereas rain is both for the righteous and for the wicked.'[3]

Love of neighbour in this period of 'new Jewish sensitivity' came to be seen as a precondition of reconciliation with God. Flusser argues that 'the best summary of this new Jewish ethics is found in the *Wisdom of Jesus the Son of Sirach* (27:30–28:7)'.[4] This passage should be read carefully:

> Anger and wrath, these also are abominations,
>   yet a sinner holds on to them.
> The vengeful will face the Lord's vengeance,
>   for he keeps a strict account of their sins.
> Forgive your neighbour the wrong he has done,
>   and then your sins will be pardoned when you pray.
> Does anyone harbour anger against another,
>   and expect healing from the Lord?
> If someone has no mercy towards another like himself,
>   can he then seek pardon for his own sins?
> If a mere mortal harbours wrath,
>   who will make an atoning sacrifice for his sins?

Remember the end of your life, and set enmity aside;
  remember corruption and death, and be true to the
  commandments.
Remember the commandments, and do not be angry with your
  neighbour;
  remember the covenant of the Most High, and overlook faults.
                                                   (Eccles. 27.30—28.7)

Jesus the son of Sirach lived around 200 BCE. As can be seen, his words surely confirm that Flusser is correct to say that Jesus of Nazareth stood in a strong, continuous stream of Jewish thought. This thesis is strengthened by the close parallels between the famous Pharisee, Hillel (died *c*.10 CE), and Jesus in respect of the so-called golden rule: 'In everything do to others as you would have them do to you; for this is the law and the prophets' (Matt. 7.12); 'What is distasteful to yourself, do not do to your neighbour; that is the whole law, the rest is commentary.'[5]

The parallel speaks for itself. That said, Jesus turned Hillel's negative form of the golden rule into a positive injunction. He encouraged his followers not simply to refrain from doing to others what they would not want done to them, they were to be proactive and do to others what they would like for themselves. This supports Flusser's contention that the creative genius of Jesus is seen in that he 'went further and broke the last fetters still restricting the ancient Jewish commandment to love one's neighbor'.[6] This is what makes him stand out from others:

> The commandment to love one's enemies is so much his definitive characteristic that his only are the lips from which we hear the commandment in the whole of the New Testament. Elsewhere we hear only of mutual love, and blessing one's persecutors. In those days it was obviously very difficult for people to rise up to the heights of Jesus' commandment.[7]

Flusser finds integrity between Jesus' 'total way of life' and 'the purpose of his message':

He who avoided his parental home in Nazareth and became the 'friend of publicans and sinners' felt himself sent to 'the lost sheep of the house of Israel' ... From the beginning until his death on the cross, the preaching of Jesus was, in turn, linked so much with his own way of life.[8]

For Flusser, this is one of the keys to making sense of the impact of Jesus' life and message:

Those who listened to Jesus' preaching of love might well have been moved by it. Many in those days thought as he did. Nonetheless, in the clear purity of his love they must have detected something very special. Jesus did not accept all that was thought and taught in the Judaism of his time. Although not really a Pharisee himself, he was closest to the Pharisees of the school of Hillel who preached love, but he pointed the way further to unconditional love – even of one's enemies and of sinners ... this was no sentimental doctrine.[9]

Question for reflection or discussion

- How much allowance do you make for Jesus being a Jewish man who was influenced by the best sages and scholars of his people?[10]

I agree wholeheartedly with Flusser. Jesus both stood in the stream of the best teaching of his people and also 'pushed the envelope', breaking new ground in his challenge that his followers 'love' their enemies. In chapters 6 and 7 I will ask, 'How did Jesus come to take this radical stance?' But in the remainder of this chapter, we will survey a range of perspectives of scholars, of various creeds and backgrounds, about this teaching of Jesus, some of whom do not hold such a high view of Jesus as David Strauss and David Flusser.

What others have said about Jesus' teaching about the love of enemies

Claude Montefiore (1858–1938)

Claude Montefiore was a British Jewish scholar and spiritual leader of liberal persuasion. Against the background of the terrible history of Jewish–Christian relations, Gregory Barker describes Montefiore as a Jew who travelled as far as might be possible in terms of giving Jesus a positive evaluation.[11]

Montefiore, writing in 1927, places Jesus in the esteemed company of the prophets.[12] In a later work he offered the following observation about Jesus' command to love the enemy:

> my verdict would be that Jesus unites himself with the *very* best Rabbinic teaching of his own and later times. It is, perhaps, only in the trenchancy and eager intensity that he goes beyond it. There is a fire, a passion, an intensity, a broad and deep positiveness, about these verses which is new. Jesus suffers no exceptions.[13]

So Montefiore anticipated Flusser's stance. However, he also asked if Jesus or any of his followers actually succeeded in completely fulfilling this injunction. With Jesus' stinging criticisms of the scribes and Pharisees in mind (Matt. 23), Montefiore wrote:

> how much more telling his (*sc.* Jesus') injunction would have been if we had a *single story* about his doing good to, and praying for a single Rabbi or Pharisee! One grain of practice is worth a pound of theory.[14]

My response would be to point Montefiore to the words of Christ on the cross: 'Father, forgive them; for they do not know what they are doing' (Luke 23.34). However, Montefiore regards this as a prayer limited to the people who carried out the execution itself.

Joseph Klausner (1874–1958)

The second Jewish interpreter to whom we turn is Joseph Klausner, a prominent Jewish scholar in the same generation as Montefiore. His appraisal of Jesus is much more critical. Klausner was a professor of Hebrew Literature at the University of Jerusalem from 1925, and the chief editor of *The Hebrew Encyclopedia*. He was an ardent Zionist polemicist and stood as a candidate for president in the first Israeli presidential election in 1949, losing to Chaim Weizmann by 83 votes to 15. So Klausner's world view was shaped by the Holocaust and the post-war determination of Jewish people never to place themselves at the mercy of Gentiles.

Little wonder, then, that Klausner regards Jesus and his teaching about the love of the enemy as not simply impractical but positively dangerous. He 'sensed that the exaggerated Judaism represented by Jesus did not help sustain Jews in the Second Temple period and was largely irrelevant for contemporary Jews concerned with strengthening Judaism in a hostile world'.[15] Klausner wrote:

> What room is there in the world for justice if we must extend both our cheeks to our assailants and give the thief both coat and cloak? Human civilisation is wholly based on the difference between man and nature, between human society and the brute beast and vegetable world; it is, therefore, neither possible nor seemly for man to become as 'the lilies of the field' or 'the fowls of the air'.[16]

Klausner's point of view would find many adherents in today's Israel.

Ghulam Ahmad Parwez (1903–85)

We turn now to the thought of a prominent Muslim. Ghulam Ahmad Parwez was a prolific and influential Islamic thinker. His interpretation of the Qur'an was inspirational for Muhammad Ali Jinnah, the founding President of Pakistan:

Christianity favours the policy of non-resistance to evil. We are advised by it not to return evil for evil, not to meet violence with violence. The New Testament tells us that the proper answer to an act of violence is an act of love ... [cites Matt. 5.38–41] To do good in return for evil is said to be the best way to fight evil. No doubt, these are noble sentiments and in the lives of individuals may be praiseworthy. But it is doubtful if Jesus (peace be upon him) could have taught these precepts for universal behaviour; for experience does not prove their wisdom. They hold good in rare instances only, and *Anbiya* [plural of 'Prophet'] do not speak for rare exceptions. The history of Christianity too negates their authenticity ... Even in the New Testament, as it exists today, there are statements here and there which are clearly at variance with the creed of non-violence and absolute resistance to evil ... [cites Matt. 10.34–35] It is obvious that the use of force to defend a good cause is not ruled out in Christianity.[17]

So this leading Muslim questions whether Jesus really said it, and if he did, then Parwez says it must have been highly specific circumstances in which it applied. Parwez was of course thinking all this through in the context of the end of British colonial rule in India, and he was doing so alongside the influential Hindu leader, Gandhi, to whom we now turn.

Mohandas Karamchand Gandhi (1869–1948)

Gandhi, who is revered as the Father of India, was renowned for his reverence for Jesus' teaching about non-violence towards the persecutor. Indeed, you might say that he developed a policy based upon it in order to remove British rule from India.

What, then, does Jesus mean to me? To me He was one of the greatest teachers humanity has ever had ... Jesus' own life is the key of His nearness to God; that He expressed, as no other could, the spirit and will of God. It is in this sense that I see Him and recognize Him as the Son of God.[18]

In his article, 'The Jesus I love and My reaction to Christianity', Gandhi wrote:

I saw that the Sermon on the Mount was the whole of Christianity for him who wanted to live a Christian life. It is that Sermon which has endeared Jesus to me . . . I may say that I have never been interested in a historical Jesus. I should not care if it was proved by someone that the man called Jesus never lived, and that what was narrated in the Gospels was a figment of the writer's imagination. For the Sermon on the Mount would still be true for me . . . Christianity has yet to be lived.[19]

For Gandhi, the teaching of 'non-retaliation' or 'non-resistance to evil' was the thing that remained with him forever:

Jesus came almost to give a new law – though He of course said He had not come to give a new law, but tack something on to old Mosaic law. Well, He changed it so that it became a new law – not an eye for an eye, and a tooth for a tooth, but to be ready to receive two blows when one was given, and to go two miles when you were asked to go one.[20]

Tenzin Gyatso, the 14th Dalai Lama (1935–)

We turn now to a Buddhist who has engaged with Jesus' injunctions, the present Dalai Lama, Tenzin Gyatso. He writes:

The practice of tolerance and patience, which is being advocated in these passages is extremely similar to the practice of tolerance and patience which is advocated in Buddhism in general. And this is particularly true in Mahayana Buddhism in the context of the *bodhisattva ideals*.

He continues, however, to suggest that these ideals can only be lived out if we locate ourselves within a spiritual discipline:

I feel that the Gospel especially emphasises the practice of tolerance and feelings of impartiality towards all creatures. In my opinion, in order to develop one's capacity for tolerance toward all beings, and particularly toward an enemy, it is an important precondition to have a feeling of equanimity toward all. If someone tells you that you should be hostile toward your enemy or that you should love your enemy, that statement alone is not going to move you to change. It is quite natural for all of us to feel hostility toward those who harm us, and to feel attachment toward our loved ones. It is a natural human feeling, so we must have effective techniques to help us make that transition from these inherently biased feelings toward a state of greater equanimity.[21]

Clearly the Dalai Lama has in mind the disciplines of meditation and prayer within the Buddhist tradition. However, his reference to disciplines that would enable someone to follow Jesus' teaching naturally leads to my final example: Martin Luther King Jr.

Martin Luther King Jr (1929–68)

Martin Luther King and Gandhi shared similar perspectives on non-violent resistance towards oppressive forces. Indeed, Gandhi is mentioned in this famous sermon entitled 'Loving Your Enemies' delivered at Dexter Avenue Baptist Church on 17 November 1957.[22]

King begins his address by speaking of a discipline that he sought to follow:

I try to make it something of a custom or tradition to preach from this passage of scripture at least once a year, adding new insights that I develop along the way, out of new experiences as I give these messages.

He was aware that many have said that Jesus was asking something beyond our capacity to deliver:

Now let me hasten to say that Jesus was very serious when he gave this command; he wasn't playing. He realized that it's hard to love your enemies. He realized that it's difficult to love those persons who seek to defeat you, those persons who say evil things about you. He realized that it was painfully hard, pressingly hard. But he wasn't playing.

King advocated various disciplines that he considers to be vital steps toward this obedience:

you must begin by analyzing self ... we must face the fact that an individual might dislike us because of something that we've done deep down in the past, some personality attribute that we possess ... A second thing that an individual must do in seeking to love his enemy is to discover the element of good in his enemy ... Another way that you love your enemy is this: when the opportunity presents itself for you to defeat your enemy, that is the time which you must not do it.

King also encouraged his hearers to separate the individual enemy from the social systems in which they might be caught up, which may cause them to be enemies:

In the final analysis, love is not this sentimental something that we talk about. It is not merely an emotional something. Love is creative, understanding goodwill for all men. It is the refusal to defeat any individual. When you rise to the level of love, of its great beauty and power, you seek only to defeat evil systems. Individuals who happen to be caught up in that system you love, but you seek to defeat the system.

Echoing the thought of C. S. Lewis about four kinds of love, this love is neither aesthetic love (*eros*) nor friendship (*philia*).

It is the word *agape*, and *agape* is more than eros. *Agape* is more than *philia*. *Agape* is something of the understanding, creative, redemptive goodwill for all men. It is a love that seeks nothing in return. It is an overflowing love, it's what theologians would call the love of God working in the lives of men. And when you rise to love on this level, you begin to love men, not because they are likeable, but because God loves them. You look at every man and you love him because you know God loves him. And he might be the worst person you've ever seen.

King now pressed his argument home by making an appeal to two strongly pragmatic arguments. First, he turns his attention to the impact of hate upon the one who hates another:

There's another reason why you should love your enemies. And that is because hate distorts the personality of the hater.

We usually think of what hate does for the individual hated or the individuals hated or the groups hated. But it is even more tragic, it is even more ruinous and injurious to the individual who hates. You just begin hating somebody, and you will begin to do irrational things. You can't see straight when you hate. You can't walk straight when you hate. You can't stand upright. Your vision is distorted. There is nothing more tragic than to see an individual whose heart is filled with hate.

Finally, King made the following powerful point – clearly a vital one in the context of the struggle for civil rights:

Now there is a final reason I think that Jesus says, 'Love your enemies.' It is this: that love has within it a redemptive power. And there is a power there that eventually transforms individuals. That's why Jesus says, 'Love your enemies.' Because if you hate your enemies, you have no way to redeem and to transform your enemies. But if you love your enemies, you will discover that at the very root of love is the power of redemption.

Questions for reflection or discussion

In this chapter we have considered a range of significant responses to Jesus' teaching that we should love our enemies.

- How do you react to the critical perspectives of the Jewish scholars Montefiore and Klausner?
- To what extent do you agree with Klausner and Parwez that this teaching about the love of the enemy is unwise and unrealistic as a basis for state law?
- How far was Gandhi fortunate that his policy of non-violent resistance was aimed at the British Empire and not the Third Reich?
- Following the lead of the Dalai Lama and Martin Luther King Jr, what disciplines would you encourage us to adopt if we are to fulfil Jesus' challenge?

6

Jesus challenged at the boundaries

<hr>

Introduction

So far we have considered:

- Jesus' home in Nazareth;
- Jesus' annual journey with his family as they went on pilgrimage to Jerusalem;
- Jesus' incredible challenge that we should love our enemies.

I want now to press the following questions:

- How did Jesus get to think like this?
- Why did he encourage his followers to take a step that was so radical and also so difficult to do?

As we consider these questions, I think we should take note of the cautionary words of Pope Benedict XVI, Joseph Ratzinger, who recently retired. During his papacy, remarkably, he managed to write two extensive volumes entitled *Jesus of Nazareth*, and recently completed the series with a shorter study of the infancy narratives.[1]

Benedict consistently suggests that we cannot hope to comprehend Jesus if we do not take into consideration his intimate relationship with God. Jesus is the 'second Moses', who 'conversed with the Lord "face to face"; as a man speaks to his friend'.[2] 'If we are to truly understand the figure of Jesus as it is presented to us in the New Testament', we must begin by seeing that in 'Jesus the promise of the new prophet is fulfilled'. Jesus, writes Benedict, 'lives before the face of God, not just as a friend, but as a Son; he lives in the most intimate unity with the Father'.[3]

For Benedict, this brings some limitations on the fruitfulness of asking the kind of questions that I posed above. A clear example of his reticence is expressed in his discussion of the baptism of Jesus:

> A broad current of liberal scholarship has interpreted Jesus' Baptism as a vocational experience. After having led a per- fectly normal life in the province of Galilee, at the moment of his Baptism he is said to have had an earth-shattering experience. It was then, we are told, that he became aware of his special relationship with God and his religious mission ... But none of this can be found in the texts ... The texts give us no window into Jesus' inner life – Jesus stands above our psychologizing.[4]

If Pope Benedict is correct, then my questions about Jesus cannot be addressed – we simply cannot ask how Jesus came to stand out from all the other Jewish teachers or rabbis of his day by calling upon his followers to take this extra step of loving the enemy.

My answer may be simplistic, but it seems to me that we should take just as seriously the humanity of Jesus, allowing space for Jesus to grow and develop, as Pope Benedict does the divinity of Jesus. Therefore we must press the question of how Jesus came to know not simply of his sonship but also how he came to see that the Lord God required him and his disciples to love their enemies.

Questions for reflection or discussion

- Where do you stand in respect of the two views expressed above?
- What do you think are the strengths and drawbacks of the two perspectives?

Encountering a leper

Read the following passage from Mark:

> A leper came to him begging him, and kneeling he said to him, 'If you choose, you can make me clean.' Moved with pity, Jesus stretched out his hand and touched him, and said to him, 'I do choose. Be made clean!' Immediately the leprosy left him, and he was made clean. After sternly warning him he sent him away at once, saying to him, 'See that you say nothing to anyone; but go, show yourself to the priest, and offer for your cleansing what Moses commanded, as a testimony to them.' But he went out and began to proclaim it freely, and to spread the word, so that Jesus could no longer go into a town openly, but stayed out in the country; and people came to him from every quarter. (Mark 1.40–45)

You might also want to spend some time in quiet contemplation of the mosaic from Monreale Cathedral in Sicily.[5]

- How does the mosaic convey the horror of the illness with which the man suffers?
- What strikes you about the portrayal of Jesus in the mosaic?

This is the first account in Mark's Gospel of an encounter by Jesus with someone suffering with leprosy. The majority of Greek witnesses of Mark's text recall that Jesus responded with 'compassion' to the man's request for healing (v. 41). The Greek text reads *splangchnistheis*, which is a verb connected to the deep feelings associated with the bowels, *splangchna*. The ancient intuition was to associate bodily organs with particular human emotions or activities. We are not so different – in our society we talk about loving people with all of our heart. To people in Jesus' day, both Jewish and Greek, the heart was both the seat of our feelings and also of our thinking – see, for example, Judges 5.16; Psalm 10.6; and Mark 2.6. But very often the deepest feelings were thought to be derived from the guts – we still connect with this idea in such expressions as 'gut-wrenching' and 'visceral'.

The picture of Jesus being filled with compassion for the man's plight is one that resonates with us, especially when connected with a passionate plea for help from someone who was so desperate. Mark seems to underline this with the use of two verbs – 'begging' and 'kneeling', although the second verb is not in all the ancient manuscripts. However, much more perplexing is the possibility that Jesus' motive for healing the man was anger. One key manuscript from the late fourth century, Codex Bezae, has a strange and difficult reading – *orgistheis*, 'being filled with anger'. This codex, which is one of our oldest, was probably from Beirut and is bilingual, and has an equivalent Latin reading – *iratus*. Odd though this may be, many scholars take this to be the original tradition because it is harder to see how a scribe might change the motive for the healing from compassion to anger, than the other way around.[6]

A specialist who has vigorously presented this view is Bart D. Ehrman.[7] Not everyone agrees. For example, recently Peter J. Williams has argued cogently that *orgistheis* was introduced by mistake in the copying process.[8]

For me, the motive of anger fits well with the tone of the subsequent dismissal of the man: 'After sternly warning him he sent him away at once' (v. 43). The Greek verb for the stern warning is *embrimaomai*, which carries more than a hint of displeasure and anger. It is, for example, used to depict the murmuring of the disciples in Mark 14.5 at the alleged wastefulness of the woman who poured expensive ointment on Jesus' head. Thus, Lamar Williamson Jr suggests that Mark 1.43 would be better rendered as: 'he snorted at him and cast him out'.[9]

But what exactly might have caused Jesus to be irate and to bristle with such indignation? Various suggestions have been made. For example, the hostility could have been aroused by his sensing the presence of evil spirits and the perception that they were responsible for the terrible state of the man's health. If this were the case, then Jesus may have felt that he needed to go on an all-out attack. Alternatively, it may be that Jesus was piqued by the presence of hard-hearted people, perhaps even the unfortunate man himself. Ehrman thinks that the element of doubt implicit in the man's plea rankled Jesus. The 'if' might have been taken to imply that Jesus might be neither willing nor able to help. But none of these explanations can claim much support from the passage itself.

The context of the story is one in which Jesus was interrupted while at prayer, and we hear him state that he was keen to press on to other villages besides Capernaum to preach the good news. Perhaps he was angry because the approach of the leper interrupts him from this task, and also because he could foresee that such healings would attract great crowds and limit his movements. The main difficulty with this explanation is that from the start, Jesus' ministry is characterized in Mark as a powerful combination of words and deeds.

So the story leaves us with a puzzle. I would like to suggest that we explore how Jesus as a faithful Jew might have perceived leprosy in the light of the Torah, particularly as he seems to have had Leviticus 14 in mind as a guide when he required the man to present himself at the Temple with the requisite sacrificial offering. This was after all a society that considered skin diseases to be a serious problem. The identification of leprosy, the exclusion of lepers from society and the processes of their re-admission were all subject to strict priestly regulations (Lev. 13—14). Could it be that Jesus was vexed by his belonging to a society that placed those, like this man, suffering with leprosy at the margins of society and labelled them unclean? This is an attractive suggestion, particularly for those of us who want to regard Jesus as a radical Christ who comes to liberate or free people. However, it founders on the highly questionable proposal that Jesus was critical of the plain guidance of the Torah.

If we however think of Jesus as someone who regarded the Torah as God's word, and whose mind was shaped by it, then we ought not to be surprised if he was offended by the man's

approach. Here was someone whose illness rendered him con-
tagious, not simply in terms of illness but also in terms of holiness. Jesus may even have been anxious that this man could
potentially render him ritually unclean. So I suggest that the
incident recollects an encounter between Jesus and a significant
cultural and religious threshold. To be in the presence of a leper
meant being close to the unclean, and Jesus was not at ease with
this. Furthermore, granted that he felt that he must touch the
man to heal him (v. 41), Jesus knew that healing entailed taking
a risk. It is not difficult to imagine the inner questions that
may have flashed through his mind: 'What if the healing fails?',
'Will I become unclean?', 'Will I become leprous myself?' This
opens up a fresh understanding, then, of Jesus' vexation and
hostility. However, his risks turned out to be worthwhile – the
man was healed and the event became what I would call a
'threshold moment' both for him and for Jesus.

Questions for reflection or discussion

- When have you found yourself in a situation in which you felt
  compelled to act but did not feel ready? Does this help you
  relate to this story about Jesus?
- How do you respond to the idea that Jesus was angry when
  he healed the leprous man?

Before we move on to another significant story from the Gospels,
it is worthwhile to add that perhaps we do not have to choose
between compassion and anger as a motive for Jesus' healing in
this story – deep feelings can often be a mixture of both anger
and compassion. Some scholars have also noted that Jesus did
not speak Greek but Aramaic, and have wondered if behind both
readings, *splangchnistheis* and *orgistheis*, lies an Aramaic verb,
such as *regaz*, that conveyed both nuances.[10] If this is correct,
then we do not have to choose between the two motives.

Encountering a persistent Phoenician mother

Read the following passage from Mark:

> From there he set out and went away to the region of Tyre. He entered a house and did not want anyone to know he was there. Yet he could not escape notice, but a woman whose little daughter had an unclean spirit immediately heard about him, and she came and bowed down at his feet. Now the woman was a Gentile, of Syrophoenician origin. She begged him to cast the demon out of her daughter. He said to her, 'Let the children be fed first, for it is not fair to take the children's food and throw it to the dogs.' But she answered him, 'Sir, even the dogs under the table eat the children's crumbs.' Then he said to her, 'For saying that, you may go – the demon has left your daughter.' So she went home, found the child lying on the bed, and the demon gone.
>
> (Mark 7.24–30)

Everyone needs a holiday – even Jesus did. His trip to Tyre was a seaside break from his Galilean ministry; it may also have been linked to his need to lie low, away from Antipas' spies. Away in 'pagan' territory, where he was not a household name or a celebrity, Jesus was hoping for some 'R & R', and time perhaps to consider the next steps in his mission and ministry. But as we all know, when you are off duty there is just a chance something will happen that necessitates a temporary return to work. A woman whose daughter was ill got wind that a healer was in town, and before long she was at his lodgings pleading for help. What followed is a dialogue that is brusque but also very revealing.

Jesus does not reply by saying, 'I am on holiday. Call me when I am back at the office.' Rather, he shockingly invokes the walls of separation between Jew and Gentile: 'Let the children be fed first, for it is not fair to take the children's food and throw it to the dogs.' This is classic Jewish thinking about Gentiles – they were the 'uncircumcised', the dogs who did not discriminate what they ate! It surely was part of Jesus' outlook

85

as a Jewish man, and chimes in with a Jesus who did not see himself as having a mission to Gentiles. Indeed, Matthew tells us as much in his version of this story, which adds the saying: 'I was sent only to the lost sheep of the house of Israel' (Matt. 15.24).

Christian commentators, when they comment on this incident, are generally at pains to exonerate Jesus of charges of bigotry and racist attitudes. Perhaps, they say, Jesus was being deliberately provocative so as to evoke faith on the part of this mother – he did not mean what he said but was playing a psychological game so as to draw more from her. Alternatively, Jesus is considered here to be taking the opportunity to teach his disciples something new – voicing typical Jewish attitudes so that his disciples could recognize their inadequacy.

Laudable though these lines of interpretation may be, they leave little room for the possibility of growth in the person of Jesus. Further, they rob us of the extraordinary insight that Jesus learned from his conversation with this Gentile woman that God has bread for Gentiles too. In other words, this encounter also encapsulates a 'threshold moment' for Jesus as well as for the woman. The dialogue between Jesus and this importunate woman leads him to a new place, to a widening of his horizons and to a change of heart.

Question for reflection or discussion

• How do you respond to the idea that Jesus might have warranted the equivalent of an eight-match suspension for inappropriate references to the woman's ethnicity?

Spend some time either singing or reading the following hymn by John M. Campbell, which explores poetically the ideas suggested above. It can be sung to the tunes of Penlan ('In Heavenly Love Abiding') or Aurelia ('The Church's One Foundation').

Unwanted interruption
Disturbing hard won peace;
A pressure put upon you
Just when you'd found release;
This woman and her anguish
Intrude with honest pain,
Demanding understanding –
Though, seemingly, in vain.

Did pressures of the moment
Prevent a kind reply –
Upwellings of raw anger
Resist, refuse, deny?
Or did your people's story
Of holiness apart
Constrict your way of seeing,
Exclude her from the start?

Still, somehow, all undaunted,
She would not be denied –
No sharp-tongued, bitter rudeness
Could push her hope aside.
Persistently and wisely,
She turned your words around;
She cut through your resistance,
Claimed crumbs could still be found.

And so two healings happened –
Her daughter was set free –
But with new understanding
you surely came to see
that grace and loving kindness,
if true to what God meant,
must reach to all who need them,
show limitless intent.

Thank God, then, for that woman
And what she did for you,
The healing she enabled
Must touch us, change us too.
When prejudiced or stubborn,
Or drained of all our good,
Then may we too know healing,
To live the way we should.[11]

Encountering 'living death'

Read the following passage from Mark:

And a large crowd followed him and pressed in on him. Now there was a woman who had been suffering from haemorrhages for twelve years. She had endured much under many physicians, and had spent all that she had; and she was no better, but rather grew worse. She had heard about Jesus, and came up behind him in the crowd and touched his cloak, for she said, 'If I but touch his clothes, I will be made well.' Immediately her haemorrhage stopped; and she felt in her body that she was healed of her disease. Immediately aware that power had gone forth from him, Jesus turned about in the crowd and said, 'Who touched my clothes?' And his disciples said to him, 'You see the crowd pressing in on you; how can you say, "Who touched me?"' He looked all round to see who had done it. But the woman, knowing what had happened to her, came in fear and trembling, fell down before him, and told him the whole truth. He said to her, 'Daughter, your faith has made you well; go in peace, and be healed of your disease.'

(Mark 5.24–34)

This is the final example we will consider in this chapter. By placing this story inside another story about the raising to life of a 12-year-old girl who had died, Mark wants us to see that this woman's 12 years of suffering a haemorrhage was a kind of 'living death'. Certainly, in the light of the legislation in Leviticus 15.19–30, this woman's plight excluded her from normal social interaction. The healing was therefore about much more than the healing of a physical ailment. Second, what she did placed her and Jesus at risk. Her actions, if discovered, would have necessitated that Jesus undergo some kind of cleansing ritual before entering sacred space. For her, the risks were enormous in a society that was so punitive.

The vulnerability of both the woman and Jesus has been powerfully encapsulated in a remarkable book by Sara Maitland entitled *Stations of the Cross*.[12] Maitland employs artistic licence to make the unnamed woman of Mark 5 also into the mysterious figure of Veronica, who wipes Jesus' face at the sixth station with cloth that is alleged to receive the impression of Jesus' face:

> This is my first visit to Jerusalem. I am free: I can go about in the crowd without having to take responsibility for their danger of contamination; I can walk freely in the Temple courtyards, visit with a friend, enjoy all the sites and the bustle and the tension of the streets. I can praise God in his own house, and receive guests in mine. After twelve years I am free; and I do not want to have to go back into shame.[13]

However, Veronica's attention has been grabbed by the sounds of the crowd in the streets gloating over the shame of someone on the way to crucifixion. To her horror it is Jesus: 'it is him. I cannot help remembering. His shame and the mood of the crowd are too precise, too like mine; I cannot just put aside all those twelve years and forget.' And this sets in motion a memory of that day in Capernaum, which has a remarkable symmetry with this day in Jerusalem:

> my neighbours all knew, worn out by the curse on me, I had staggered up the crowded street, just as he staggers up this one. He is bleeding; I was bleeding . . . Each time I went down to the washing-place I could see the gossips eyeing me with a delicate and half-discreet curiosity, a kind of tender fearfulness. I hated

it and I had to go; if I could have afforded to, I would have burned my soiled cloths and kept to the privacy of my own house, but untouchable, unmarriageable, defiled and defiling, always unclean . . . Twelve years. Twelve years – four thousand, three hundred and eighty days. And each morning I would have to strip off the blood-stained linen cloths and wrap on clean ones. Each morning I would examine my conscience, carefully going through each space of time across my whole life to find out what I had done that I should be so punished. There was nothing there. I was innocent.[14]

The healing, as we noted above, was brought about by a touch. But for the woman and for Jesus such a touch was not without risk:

I heard that he healed by touching. He would not touch me. I knew he would not touch me. He would ask me what healing I needed and I would have to tell him, and he would pull back, disgusted, and he would not touch me. Even if I did not tell him, someone would: they would move away from him and me, and there would be a space around us. Someone would shout out a warning and he would step back horrified, and I would be shamed. I didn't have the gall to ask him to touch me. I could not face the shame of him refusing to touch me.[15]

But when the opportunity arose the woman decided to risk all just to touch a piece of his clothing. But for Jesus, that surreptitious touch drains him: 'Immediately aware that power had gone forth from him, Jesus turned about in the crowd and said, "Who touched my clothes?"' (Mark 5.30).

Questions for reflection or discussion

- In my imagination I connect the impact of the woman's touch with what I imagine it may be like in a power station when everyone has been watching something on the TV like the opening ceremony of the Olympic Games. The event is now over. Everyone at the same moment fills their kettle and switches on to make tea. Suddenly all the power in the grid surges out, and if it is a night-time event, all the lights flicker. Was that, I wonder, how this touch felt for Jesus?

- In the stories of Jesus and the Leper, and Jesus and the Syro-phoenician woman, I suggested that the events challenged Jesus at the boundaries of his world. What might Jesus have learned from this meeting with the woman whose touch drained him? Could one lesson be that Jesus discovered he was on a path on which he was not completely in control?

- Watch Scenes 8, 'Who touched me?' and 17 'Crucifixion' of the film *The Miracle Maker*. What stands out for you from this animated reconstruction of the healing of the woman and the raising of Tamar, the daughter of Jairus? Note how the film's writer, Murray Watts, weaves the story of Tamar's healing together with the crucifixion, drawing out a similar message to Maitland's.

Some final thoughts

Underlying each story we have considered in this chapter is the other story of Jesus – as the great physician who comes to heal us at his own expense. To my mind, all these stories point to the mystery of the incarnation, and remind us of the important message of St Gregory of Nazianzus, who argued that Jesus had to be completely one with us in order to rescue and save us: 'For that which He has not assumed He has not healed; but that which is united to His Godhead is also saved.'[16] To do this, God in Christ must become vulnerable – this is of course beautifully expressed in the great poem by William Vanstone:

> Love that gives, gives ever more,
>   gives with zeal, with eager hands,
> spares not, keeps not, all outpours,
>   ventures all, its all expends.

> Drained is love in making full,
>   bound in setting others free,
> poor in making many rich,
>   weak in giving power to be.[17]

These stories also give an insight into the background to Jesus' teaching that we must love our enemies. They do so by hinting at the journey for Jesus, a struggle that leads him inexorably to the cross where he dies to reconcile enemies.

> But now in Christ Jesus you who once were far off have been brought near by the blood of Christ. For he is our peace; in his flesh he has made both groups into one and has broken down the dividing wall, that is, the hostility between us.
>
> (Eph. 2.13–14)

7

Faltering footsteps with Jesus

Introduction

In this final chapter I will be inviting you to travel onwards with Jesus, sustained by his dream of the kingdom of God, which was the hope of a world of justice and peace. The stories we will think about are connected with Shechem, which is today called Nablus. This is the place where Jesus is said to have met a Samaritan woman by a well – although in John it was called Sychar. The well, of course, does not still exist – although a reconstruction is available for pilgrims to see in the Greek Orthodox convent on the site.

Today Nablus is one of the cities at the heart of the tragic story of Israel and Palestine in our time. It was the starting point for a 36 km (22 miles) pilgrimage that I undertook on 9 April 2011 in the company of three friends, David Andrews-Brown, Keith Begg and Father John Manilayathu. David is a retired journalist whom I met at Tantur Ecumenical Institute, Jerusalem. He was about to make the journey from Nazareth to Jerusalem and welcomed our company for one leg of his pilgrimage. Keith was working for an NGO called the Israel Palestine Centre for Research and Information. Father John is an Orthodox priest from India. Like me, he was staying at Tantur for a period of sabbatical study.

Walking with the father and mother of Israel

A 36 km walk in a contested area of the world is no picnic – it was an adventure I will never forget, and one that needed good planning. There were the practicalities of keeping up a steady pace, drinking sufficient water, eating high-energy food on the way and making sure all in our party were able to keep going. Then there was the business of keeping out of trouble. This was not easy given the various checkpoints on our route that bore more than a passing resemblance to a medieval fortress, staffed by nervous, heavily armed soldiers, deeply suspicious of our motivation for making such a journey on foot.

Question for reflection or discussion

Look at the photograph in Plate 7.1. It was taken in a quiet street in the evening on a Friday in Nablus. The children's toys are tidily gathered together at the end of the day's play, under the watchful eye of iconic posters of martyrs who had died recently for the Palestinian cause.

- What do you think it is like to grow up in such a tense, bitter place?

Plate 7.1 A strange combination in Nablus
Source Photograph by the author.

On the day I found it comforting to think I might be walking where Abram and Sarai had walked. But I also wondered what the Patriarch would have made of the deep conflict between his children through Isaac, the son of Sarai (Gen. 21) and the traditional father of the Jewish people, and his children through Ishmael, the son of Hagar (Gen. 16) and the traditional father of the Arab peoples. What I do know is that Abram and Sarai would have done what they always did on their wanderings – *erected an altar to the LORD and prayed.*

Reading from the Scriptures

Abram passed through the land to the place at Shechem, to the oak of Moreh. At that time the Canaanites were in the land. Then the LORD appeared to Abram, and said, 'To your offspring I will give this land.' So he built there an altar to the LORD, who had appeared to him. From there he moved on to the hill country on the east of Bethel, and pitched his tent, with Bethel on the west and Ai on the east; and there he built an altar to the LORD and invoked the name of the LORD. (Gen. 12.6–8)

Miroslav Volf is a modern scholar who has thought deeply about the tragedy of human conflict – his book *Exclusion and Embrace* is a classic study of issues connected with identity, otherness and reconciliation. In this book Volf, as a native Croatian, reflected on his struggles with understanding how a Christian should respond to the tragedy unfolding in the Balkans in the 1990s. One key figure from Scripture that Volf identifies as crucial is Abraham. 'At the very foundation of Christian faith stands the towering figure of Abraham.'[1] Volf points out that his story begins with an abrupt call from God: 'Now the LORD said to Abram, "Go"' (Gen. 12.1). In going forth, Abram's faith was expressed in the risky business of embarking on the journey from the known – 'your country and your kindred' (Gen. 12.1) – to the unknown. There is something very important going on here in terms of Abram's identity – everything that defined him was tied with being where he was. To find his new identity he must give it all up, trusting in nothing more than the bare promise of God. Here Volf refers us to the insights of Walter Brueggemann:

> the command to 'go forth' placed before Abraham a difficult choice: he would either belong to his country, his culture, and his family and remain comfortably inconsequential or, risking everything, he would depart and become great – a blessing to 'all the families of the earth'.[2]

This characteristic, says Volf, is what marks Abraham out.

> The courage to break his cultural and familial ties and abandon the gods of his ancestors (Joshua 24:2) out of allegiance to a God of all families and all cultures was the original Abrahamic revolution.[3]

The willingness to give up belonging to a particular group, clan and nation and go to find a God who is there for all peoples seems to me to be foundational in the story of Abraham. This is how Abraham and Sarah can continue to be a source of blessing for all peoples.

Questions for reflection or discussion

- Are there places like Nablus in your life where an atmosphere of conflict is present, and in which you need to build a symbolic altar for the Lord?
- How do you respond to the idea that to follow in the footsteps of Abram and Sarai, we too must be willing to leave behind our old identities and allegiances?

What would Jesus do?

On the following day, with very sore feet, during Mass in the Latin church in Taybeh, I found myself gazing at a painting that tried to depict the encounter between Jesus and the woman from Sychar. As I did so, I reflected over a day of walking through a beautiful landscape, scarred at the superficial level by rubbish, broken glass and human detritus, but at a much deeper level by the deep divisions between Jew, Christian and Muslim, by racial division, competition and greed. And I could not help but think that the sage from Galilee, who could think outside the boundaries of his world, still holds the key to a better future for this region.

> [Jesus] left Judea and started back to Galilee. But he had to go through Samaria. So he came to a Samaritan city called Sychar, near the plot of ground that Jacob had given to his son Joseph. Jacob's well was there, and Jesus, tired out by his journey, was sitting by the well. It was about noon. A Samaritan woman came to draw water, and Jesus said to her, 'Give me a drink' . . . The Samaritan woman said to him, 'How is it that you, a Jew, ask a drink of me, a woman of Samaria?' (Jews do not share things in common with Samaritans.) . . . The woman said to him, 'Sir, I see that you are a prophet. Our ancestors worshipped on this mountain, but you say that the place where people must worship is in Jerusalem.' Jesus said to her, 'Woman, believe me, the hour is coming when you will worship the Father neither on this mountain nor in Jerusalem. You worship what you do not know; we worship what we know, for salvation is from the Jews. But the hour is coming, and is now here, when the true worshippers will worship the Father in spirit and truth, for the Father seeks such as these to worship him.'　　　(John 4.3–7, 9, 19–23)

In his commentary on John, Mark Stibbe points out that John 4 echoes 'the betrothal type-scene' in Jewish literature:

1 The bridegroom journeying to a foreign land
2 He meets a girl (or girls) at a well

3 Someone draws water from the well
4 This leads to the girl running home to announce the stranger
5 The man and woman are betrothed, generally in the context of a meal.[4]

The parallels between this passage and the stories of how Jacob met Rachel (Gen. 29) and Moses met Zipporah (Exod. 2.16–21) should be noted. Stibbe suggests that in John 4 there is a symbolic betrothal – Jesus, who is the bridegroom (John 3.29) of the Church, becomes 'the seventh man in her life', 'the man she has been waiting for, the man in whose presence she will find wholeness (*sōtēria*, v. 22)'.[5]

Whether you follow Stibbe completely or not, definite parallels between Jacob and Jesus are intended. Just as Jacob had provided the people with water (John 4.12), now Jesus comes to provide 'living water' (v. 11) from a well on the inside of a person (v. 14). Jacob's visit to Shechem had also resulted in conflict and death (Gen. 34) – violence that he repudiated and from which he distanced himself (Gen. 49.5–7). Jesus visits Sychar at a time of deep conflict between Jews and Samaritans to offer a different kind of future.

John fully reflects the shock of the woman that Jesus would even engage with a Samaritan man, let alone a woman. And in the reaction of the disciples, we sense their dismay: 'Just then his disciples came. They were astonished that he was speaking with a woman, but no one said, "What do you want?" or, "Why are you speaking with her?"' (John 4.27).

Given the parallels noted above, no wonder they got the wrong idea. We also need to bear in mind the wider attitude to social relations between men and women in the public domain, which may be reflected in the Mishnah:

Jose ben Johanan said, Let thy house be opened wide and let the needy be members of thy household; and talk not much with womankind. They said this of a man's own wife: how much more of his fellow's wife! Hence the Sages have said:

he that talks much with womankind brings evil upon himself and neglects the study of the Law and at last will inherit Gehenna.[6]

So John presents once more to us a Jesus who at risk to himself and his reputation crosses significant boundaries to meet the stranger. In this case we are considering the traversing of the barbed wire fence between a man and a woman, and the wall between Jew and Samaritan. Jesus took the initiative, 'Give me a drink', and it throws the woman completely: 'How is it that you, a Jew, ask a drink of me, a woman of Samaria?' (John 4.7, 9). This is remarkably risky. Why did Jesus take such risks and what does this encounter say to us?

The story also has something important to say about how to engage in dialogue without compromising your own integrity. Jesus takes a Jewish view of the dispute between the Samaritans and the Jews – 'You worship what you do not know; we worship what we know, for salvation is from the Jews' (v. 22). Even Jesus as incarnate son of God can only begin with the place from whence he comes. That is part of the glory of incarnation – God may have chosen in Christ to embrace the human race as a whole, but he began from the Jewish matrix, represented by his mother Mary and his adoptive father, Joseph. So Jesus enters into dialogue with the Samaritan woman owning his own culture. But he was not trapped by his own culture. In this encounter Jesus points to a new future that lies beyond the present impasse: 'Woman, believe me, the hour is coming when you will worship the Father neither on this mountain nor in Jerusalem' (v. 21).

Here Jesus reminds me of the famous aphorism of C. H. Spurgeon, 'Of two evils, choose neither.' Of course, neither the Judaism nor the Samaritanism of the day were wholly good or wholly evil, but they were locked, as we noted in Chapter 2, in an interminable conflict from which there seemed no escape. What Jesus does is reject the either/or category – he is here an advocate of the third way: Jesus seeks a new future in which Jew and Samaritan can find a new spiritual unity in a faith that transcends place and location.

This is fundamental to the revolution that Jesus brought – he had the imagination to dream of a different future for both Jew and Samaritan. Dreamers of this kind seem to me to be more needed than ever before.

Questions for reflection or discussion

- In the light of the challenges of living in a world that is multi-racial and multi-faith, how should we seek to relate to our neighbours of completely different backgrounds?
- To what extent do you agree with me that John 4 offers a pattern for polite and courteous dialogue with people of other faiths than our own?
- How will you strive to share in Jesus' dream of the reign of God?

Conclusion

We come then to the close of this book. In the first four chapters my aim was to help you imagine Jesus' world, his home and the journeys he took with his family from Nazareth to Jerusalem to celebrate the pilgrim festival of the Passover. I then sought to set in context Jesus' radical call for his followers to love their enemies, and included a range of more contemporary perspectives about this challenging teaching. My sympathies lie with Mahatma Gandhi and Martin Luther King Jr, who were committed to taking his words seriously. But I included other voices because I want to acknowledge that they do seem hopelessly idealistic in the ears of people like Joseph Klausner who have experienced atrocity and terrible injustice.

In the final two chapters my aim was to show that Jesus himself found it challenging when he encountered the key boundaries within his world and culture. He did not find it easy to cross the thresholds between the clean and the unclean, between male and female, between Jew and Gentile, between the living and those experiencing living death. Nonetheless, he did cross them, and I would suggest that he did so because of the dream that is encapsulated in his prayer to God, 'Your kingdom come, your will be done, on earth as it is in heaven.' In teaching his disciples to love their enemies, and to pray his prayer, he was encouraging them to dream God's dreams with him.

As we approach Easter once again, that is still his gift to the world. Where people cannot find a way, Jesus still comes and wants people to imagine a world that is different, to pray for that world and to work to bring it about. Here lies the hope that is needed, not just in the West Bank, but everywhere.

Conclusion

God of revelation,
Whose mercy embraces all peoples and nations:
Tear down the walls which divide us,
Break open the prisons which hold us captive
and so free us to celebrate your beauty in all the earth,
Through Jesus Christ our Redeemer. Amen.[1]

Notes

1 Jesus: his home

1 See, for example, Roberts' *View of the Convent of Terra Santa, Nazareth* (1839) at <www.jordanjubilee.com/images/droberts/photos/xnazareth.jpg>.

2 Bellarmino Bagatti, *Excavations in Nazareth*, trans. Fr Eugene Hoarde (Jerusalem: Franciscan Printing House, 1969), p. 27.

3 Andrew Mayes, *Holy Land? Challenging Questions from the Biblical Landscape* (London: SPCK, 2011), p. 37.

4 Mayes, *Holy Land?*, p. 38.

5 For a fuller account of the history of the struggle over Daheer's vineyard see <www.tentofnations.org>.

6 Bagatti, *Excavations in Nazareth*, p. 27.

7 <www.uhl.ac/en/projects/nazareth-village-project/> (accessed 19 June 2013).

8 <www.nazarethvillage.com/research/content/houses> (accessed 1 April 2011).

9 Craig Evans, *Jesus and His World: The Archaeological Evidence* (London: SPCK, 2012), p. 13.

10 Sean Freyne, *Galilee, Jesus and the Gospels* (Philadelphia: Fortress Press, 1988), p. 155.

11 Freyne, *Galilee, Jesus and the Gospels*, p. 154.

12 Jonathan Reed, 'Instability in Jesus' Galilee: A Demographic Perspective', *Journal of Biblical Literature*, vol. 129, no. 2 (2010), p. 345.

13 Reed, 'Instability in Jesus' Galilee', pp. 357–8.

14 Josephus, *Jewish Antiquities*, 17.271, 288–9.

15 Josephus, *Jewish Antiquities*, 18.27.

16 Josephus, *Jewish Antiquities*, 18.37–8.

17 Richard Horsley, *Archaeology, History and Society in Galilee: The Social Context of Jesus and the Rabbis* (Valley Forge, PA: Trinity Press International, 1996), pp. 33–4.

18 Richard A. Batey, *Jesus and the Forgotten City: New Light on Sepphoris and the Urban World of Jesus* (Grand Rapids, MI: Baker Book House 1991).

19 A full review can be read in Evans, *Jesus and His World* – see especially 'In the Shadow of Sepphoris: Growing up in Nazareth', pp. 13–37; Eric M. Meyers and Mark A. Chancey, *Alexander to Constantine: Archaeology of the Land of the Bible* (New Haven, CT and London: Yale University Press, 2012) – see especially their study of 'The Impact of Antipas', pp. 117–21, and 'The Growth of Greco-Roman Culture and the Case of Sepphoris', pp. 260–84.

20 Evans, *Jesus and His World*, p. 22.

21 Evans, *Jesus and His World*, p. 24.

2 Jesus: his journey (part 1)

1 <www.preraphaelites.org/the-collection/1896P80/the-finding-of-the-saviour-in-the-temple>.

2 <www.csj.org.uk/planning.htm>.

3 Richard Horsley, *Archaeology, History and Society in Galilee: The Social Context of Jesus and the Rabbis* (Valley Forge, PA: Trinity Press International, 1996), pp. 25–36.

4 Sean Freyne, *Galilee, Jesus and the Gospels* (Philadelphia: Fortress Press, 1988), p. 155.

5 C. S. Mann, *Mark: A New Translation with Introduction and Commentary*, Anchor Bible, vol. 27 (New York: Doubleday, 1986), p. 229.

6 Herodotus, *History*, IV, 79–80, 108.

7 Eric M. Meyers and Mark A. Chancey, *Alexander to Constantine: Archaeology of the Land of the Bible* (New Haven, CT and London: Yale University Press, 2012), p. 249.

8 Josephus, *Jewish War*, 2.366.

9 Freyne, *Galilee, Jesus and the Gospels*, p. 185.

10 There are various scholarly resources available about the Samaritans for those who would like to look more deeply into the background to this conflict. For example: John Bowman, *Samaritan Documents: Relating to their History, Religion and Life* (Pennsylvania: Pickwick Press, 1977); Richard Coggins, *Samaritans and Jews: The Origins of*

Samaritanism Reconsidered (Oxford: Blackwell, 1975); John Macdonald, *The Theology of the Samaritans* (London: SCM Press, 1964); Yitzhak Magan, 'Bells, Pendants, Snakes and Stones: A Samaritan Temple to the Lord on Mt. Gerizim', *Biblical Archaeological Review* 36.6, 2010, pp. 26–35, 70; Reinhard Plummer, *The Samaritans* (Leiden: Brill, 1987).

11 Plummer, *The Samaritans*, p. 3. Note that *halakah* means 'way of walking', and refers to the ethical instruction developed by the rabbis; *aggadah* means 'legend'; that is, a story told for the same purpose.

12 Plummer, *The Samaritans*, p. 3. The Samaritan account can be found in *The Samaritan Chronicle, or The Book of Joshua the Son of Nun* (chapter 43), trans. O. T. Crane (New York: Joh. R. Alden, 1890).

13 Gerd Theissen and Annette Merz, *The Historical Jesus: A Comprehensive Guide* (London: SCM Press, 1998), p. 178.

3 Jesus: his journey (part 2)

1 Josephus, *Jewish War*, 3.44–7.

2 Josephus, *Jewish War*, 2.59.

3 Josephus, *Jewish Antiquities*, 18.27.

4 Josephus, *Jewish War*, 1.408–14; *Jewish Antiquities*, 15.331–41; 16.136–41.

5 Eric M. Meyers and Mark A. Chancey, *Alexander to Constantine: Archaeology of the Land of the Bible* (New Haven, CT and London: Yale University Press, 2012), p. 64.

6 Image at <en.wikipedia.org/wiki/File:Livia_statue.jpg>.

7 Josephus, *Jewish Antiquities*, 17.342–8.

8 Lester Grabbe, *Judaism from Cyrus to Hadrian* (London: SCM Press, 1992), p. 423.

9 Josephus, *Jewish War*, 4.452–3.

10 Sean Freyne, *Galilee, Jesus and the Gospels* (Philadelphia: Fortress Press, 1988), pp. 186–7.

4 Jerusalem, journey's end

1 This can be seen at <www.victorianweb.org/painting/lear/paintings/3.html>.

2 Josephus, *Jewish War*, 5.136–9.
3 Ronnie Reich, Gideon Avni and Tamar Winter, *The Jerusalem Archaeological Park*; rev. edn (Jerusalem: Israel Antiquities Authority, 1999), p. 230.
4 Josephus, *Jewish War*, 5.222–4.
5 Eric M. Meyers and Mark A. Chancey, *Alexander to Constantine: Archaeology of the Land of the Bible* (New Haven, CT and London: Yale University Press, 2012), pp. 59–60.
6 Josephus, *Jewish War*, 6.423–5.
7 Josephus, *Jewish War*, 2.280.
8 Joachim Jeremias, *Jerusalem in the Time of Jesus* (London: SCM Press, 1969), pp. 82–4.
9 Tacitus, *History*, 5.13.
10 See further E. P. Sanders, *Judaism: Practice and Belief 63 BCE–66 CE* (London: SCM Press, 1992), pp. 126–8.
11 Mishnah, *Aboth*, 5.5.
12 Jeremias, *Jerusalem in the Time of Jesus*, p. 71.
13 Peter Richardson, *Herod: King of the Jews and Friend of the Romans* (Columbia, SC: University of South Carolina Press, 1996), p. 180.
14 Josephus, *Jewish War*, 5.161–75.
15 Josephus, *Jewish War*, 5.176–81.
16 Josephus, *Jewish War*, 5.182–3.
17 Mishnah, *Eduyoth*, 1.3.
18 Mishnah, *Baba Bathra*, 2.9.
19 Jeremias, *Jerusalem in the Time of Jesus*, p. 9.
20 Jeremias, *Jerusalem in the Time of Jesus*, p. 93.
21 Sanders, *Judaism: Practice and Belief*, p. 147.
22 Jeremias, *Jerusalem in the Time of Jesus*, p. 9.
23 Jeremias, *Jerusalem in the Time of Jesus*, pp. 19–20.
24 Mishnah, *Kelim*, 1.6–9.
25 Translation from Craig Evans, *Jesus and His World: The Archaeological Evidence* (London: SPCK, 2012), p. 91.
26 *Papyrus Oxyrhynchus* 840, trans. in Evans, *Jesus and His World*, p. 93.
27 For further study of ritual immersion, see the following: the Mishnah (the tractate *Mikwaoth*, 'Immersion Pools'), trans. Herbert

Danby (Oxford: Oxford University Press, 1933), pp. 732–45; Meyers and Chancey, *Alexander to Constantine*, pp. 47–9; E. P. Sanders, *Jewish Law from Jesus to the Mishnah: Five Studies* (London: SCM Press, 1990), pp. 29–31, 214–27; *Judaism: Practice and Belief 63 BCE–66 CE* (London: SCM Press, 1992), pp. 214–30.

28 See the photograph in Evans, *Jesus and His World*, p. 106.

29 K. C. Hanson and Douglas E. Oakman, *Palestine in the Time of Jesus: Social Structures and Social Conflicts* (Minneapolis, MN: Fortress Press, 1998), p. 143.

30 Josephus, *Jewish Antiquities*, 18.60 and *Jewish War*, 2.293.

31 Josephus, *Jewish Antiquities*, 7.363–67.

32 *Letter of Aristeas*, 92–5, trans. R. J. H. Shutt, in J. H. Charlesworth, *The Old Testament Pseudepigrapha*, vol. 2 (Garden City, NY: Doubleday, 1985).

33 See *Letter of Aristeas*, 90, for a description of how the blood of the sacrificial victims ran away via a special system of drains.

34 For further study about Jerusalem and the Temple in the first century CE, see the excellent discussion about the combination of practical, religious and political realities of running the Temple in 'Was Bigger Better?', in Hanson and Oakman, *Palestine in the Time of Jesus*, pp. 131–59, and the fascinating reflection about both the experience of being a first- and twenty-first-century pilgrim visiting the Temple site in 'Holy Ground', in Bruce N. Fisk, *A Hitchhiker's Guide to Jesus* (Grand Rapids, MI: Baker Academic, 2011), pp. 201–6.

35 *Jerusalem Shabbath*, 15 d.

36 Gerd Theissen and Annette Merz, *The Historical Jesus: A Comprehensive Guide* (London: SCM Press, 1998), pp. 178–9.

37 Josephus, *Jewish Antiquities*, 13.337; *Life*, 112f., 148–54, 158; *Jewish War*, 2.634; Sean Freyne, *Galilee, Jesus and the Gospels* (Philadelphia: Fortress Press, 1988), pp. 208–9.

38 Jeremias, *Jerusalem in the Time of Jesus*, pp. 63–4.

39 Sanders, *Judaism: Practice and Belief*, p. 138.

40 Josephus, *Jewish War*, 2.10–13.

41 Josephus, *Jewish War*, 2.224.

42 Josephus, *Jewish War*, 2.227; *Jewish Antiquities*, 20.112.

43 Josephus, *Jewish War*, 5.238–45.

5 Jesus: his challenge

1 David Strauss, *A New Life of Jesus*, vol. 1 (London: Williams & Norgate, 1865), p. 279.

2 David Flusser, *The Sage from Galilee* (Grand Rapids, MI/Cambridge: Eerdmans, 2007), p. 55.

3 *B. Ta'anit*, 7a, trans. Isidore Epstein – see <halakhah.com/pdf/moed/Taanith.pdf>.

4 Flusser, *The Sage from Galilee*, p. 57.

5 Hillel in *B. Shabbat*, 31a, trans. Epstein – see <halakhah.com/shabbath/shabbath_31.html>.

6 Flusser, *The Sage from Galilee*, p. 60.

7 Flusser, *The Sage from Galilee*, p. 61.

8 Flusser, *The Sage from Galilee*, p. 61.

9 David Flusser, *Jesus* (New York: Herder & Herder, 1969), cited in Gregory A. Barker and Stephen E. Gregg (eds), *Jesus Beyond Christianity: The Classic Texts* (Oxford: Oxford University Press, 2010), p. 68.

10 Should you want to look more deeply into this subject, an excellent recent essay, and good place to start, is Markus Bockmuehl, 'God's life as a Jew: Remembering the Son of God', in Beverly Roberts Gaventa and Richard B. Hays (eds), *Seeking the Identity of Jesus: A Pilgrimage* (Grand Rapids, MI/Cambridge: Eerdmans, 2008), pp. 60–78.

11 Barker and Gregg, *Jesus Beyond Christianity*, p. 46.

12 Claude Montefiore, *The Synoptic Gospels*, 2nd edn (London: Macmillan, 1927), p. cxx.

13 Claude Montefiore, *Rabbinic Literature and Gospel Teachings* (London: Macmillan, 1930), p. 103.

14 Montefiore, *Rabbinic Literature and Gospel Teachings*, p. 103.

15 Barker and Gregg, *Jesus Beyond Christianity*, pp. 52–3.

16 Barker and Gregg, *Jesus Beyond Christianity*, p. 58.

17 Barker and Gregg, *Jesus Beyond Christianity*, pp. 128–9.

18 Barker and Gregg, *Jesus Beyond Christianity*, pp. 186–7.

19 Barker and Gregg, *Jesus Beyond Christianity*, p. 189.

20 Barker and Gregg, *Jesus Beyond Christianity*, p. 189.

21 Barker and Gregg, *Jesus Beyond Christianity*, pp. 258–9.

22 All citations are from <mlk-kpp01.stanford.edu/primarydocuments/Vol4/17-Nov-1957_LovingYourEnemies.pdf>.

6 Jesus challenged at the boundaries

1 Joseph Ratzinger, Pope Benedict XVI, *Jesus of Nazareth: Part 1: From the Baptism in the Jordan to the Transfiguration*, trans. Adrian J. Walker (London: Bloomsbury, 2007); *Jesus of Nazareth: Part 2: From the Entrance into Jerusalem to the Resurrection*, trans. Philip J. Whitmore (London: Catholic Truth Society/San Francisco: Ignatius Press, 2011); *Jesus of Nazareth: The Infancy Narratives*, trans. Philip J. Whitmore (London: Bloomsbury, 2012).

2 Ratzinger, *Jesus of Nazareth: Part 1*, p. 4.

3 Ratzinger, *Jesus of Nazareth: Part 1*, p. 6.

4 Ratzinger, *Jesus of Nazareth: Part 1*, p. 24.

5 See <www.thejoyofshards.co.uk/visits/sicily/monreale/thumbnails.shtml> (Image 67).

6 To learn more about Codex Bezae, see <http://cudl.lib.cam.ac.uk/view/MS-NN-00002-00041/1>. On this site David Parker provides information about the codex and its background.

7 Bart D. Ehrman, *Misquoting Jesus: The Story Behind Who Changed the Bible and Why* (New York: Harper SanFrancisco, 2005), pp. 133–9.

8 Peter J. Williams, 'An Examination of Ehrman's Case for ὀργισθείς in Mark 1:41', *Novum Testamentum*, vol. 54, no. 1, 2012, pp. 1–12.

9 Lamar Williamson, Jr, *Mark* (Louisville, KY: John Knox Press, 1983), p. 59.

10 Maurice Casey, *Jesus of Nazareth* (London/New York: T. & T. Clark, 2010), p. 63.

11 Churches Together in Britain and Ireland, 'Being an Inclusive Church . . . and not an Exclusive Club', Racial Justice Sunday, 9 September 2012, Resource Pack, at <www.ctbi.org.uk/pdf_view.php?id=802>, pp. 7–8. Used with the permission of John Campbell.

12 Sara Maitland, *Stations of the Cross* (London: Continuum, 2009).

13 Maitland, *Stations of the Cross*, p. 51.

14 Maitland, *Stations of the Cross*, pp. 51–2.

15 Maitland, *Stations of the Cross*, pp. 52–3.

16 Saint Gregory Nazianzen, Epistle 51, to Cledonius (First Epistle against Apollinarius), in trans. C. G. Browne and J. E. Swallow, *Cyril of Jerusalem: Catechetical Lectures, Gregory of Naziansum: Orations, Sermons, Letters, Prolegomena*, Nicene and Post-Nicene

Fathers, 2nd series, vol. 7 (Buffalo, NY: Christian Literature Publishing Co., 1894), p. 440.

17 From 'Morning glory, starlit sky', by W. H. Vanstone, in *Love's Endeavour, Love's Expense: The Response of Being to the Love of God* (London: Darton, Longman & Todd, 1977), p. 119. Reproduced by permission of Darton, Longman & Todd.

7 Faltering footsteps with Jesus

1 Miroslav Volf, *Exclusion and Embrace: Theological Exploration of Identity, Otherness and Reconciliation* (Nashville, TN: Abingdon Press, 1996), p. 38.

2 Volf, *Exclusion and Embrace*, p. 38, quoting from Walter Brueggemann, *The Land: Place as Gift, Promise and Challenge in Biblical Faith* (Philadelphia: Fortress Press, 1977), pp. 15ff.

3 Volf, *Exclusion and Embrace*, p. 39.

4 Mark Stibbe, *John* (Sheffield: JSOT Press, 1993), p. 68.

5 Stibbe, *John*, p. 68.

6 Mishnah, *Aboth*, 1.5.

Conclusion

1 Prayer for Midday on Monday, from *Celebrating Common Prayer* (London: Mowbray, 1992). Reproduced by permission. Copyright © The European Province of the Society of Saint Francis 1992.

Select bibliography

Bagatti, Fr Bellarmino, *Excavations in Nazareth*, trans. Fr Eugene Hoarde (Jerusalem: Franciscan Printing House, 1969).

Barker, Gregory A. and Stephen E. Gregg (eds), *Jesus Beyond Christianity: The Classic Texts* (Oxford: Oxford University Press, 2010).

Bockmuehl, Markus, 'God's life as a Jew: Remembering the Son of God', in Beverly Roberts Gaventa and Richard B. Hays (eds), *Seeking the Identity of Jesus: A Pilgrimage* (Grand Rapids, MI/Cambridge: Eerdmans, 2008).

Ehrman, Bart D., *Misquoting Jesus: The Story Behind Who Changed the Bible and Why* (New York: Harper SanFrancisco, 2005).

Evans, Craig A., *Jesus and His World: The Archaeological Evidence* (London: SPCK, 2012).

Fisk, Bruce N., *A Hitchhiker's Guide to Jesus* (Grand Rapids, MI: Baker Academic, 2012).

Flusser, David with R. Steven Notley, *The Sage from Galilee* (Grand Rapids, MI/Cambridge: Eerdmans, 2007).

Freyne, Sean, *Galilee, Jesus and the Gospels* (Philadelphia: Fortress Press, 1988).

Grabbe, L. L., *Judaism from Cyrus to Hadrian* (London: SCM Press, 1992).

Hanson, K. C. and Douglas E. Oakman, *Palestine in the Time of Jesus: Social Structures and Social Conflicts* (Minneapolis, MN: Fortress Press, 1998).

Horsley, Richard A., *Archaeology, History and Society in Galilee* (Harrisburg, PA: Trinity Press International, 1996).

Jeremias, J., *Jerusalem in the Time of Jesus* (London: SCM Press, 1969).

Maitland, Sara, *Stations of the Cross* (London: Continuum, 2009).

Mayes, Andrew D., *Holy Land? Challenging Questions from the Biblical Landscape* (London: SPCK, 2011).

Meyers, Eric M. and Mark A. Chancey, *Alexander to Constantine: Archaeology of the Land of the Bible* (New Haven, CT and London: Yale University Press, 2012).

Reed, Jonathan, 'Jesus' Galilee: A Demographic Perspective', *Journal of Biblical Literature*, vol. 129, no. 2 (2010), pp. 343–65.

Reich, Ronnie, Gideon Avni and Tamar Winter, *The Jerusalem Archaeological Park*, rev. edn (Jerusalem: Israel Antiquities Authority, 1999).

Richardson, Peter, *Herod: King of the Jews and Friend of the Romans* (Columbia, SC: University of South Carolina Press, 1996).

Sanders, E. P., *Jewish Law from Jesus to the Mishnah: Five Studies* (London: SCM Press, 1990).

Sanders, E. P., *Judaism. Practice and Belief 63 BCE – 66 CE* (London/Philadelphia: SCM Press/Trinity Press International, 1992).

Stibbe, Mark W. G., *John* (Sheffield: JSOT Press, 1993).

Theissen, Gerd and Annette Merz, *The Historical Jesus: A Comprehensive Guide* (London: SCM Press, 1998).

Volf, Miroslav, *Exclusion and Embrace: Theological Exploration of Identity, Otherness and Reconciliation* (Nashville, TN: Abingdon Press, 1996).

Williams, Peter J., 'An Examination of Ehrman's Case for ὀργισθείς in Mark 1:41', *Novum Testamentum*, vol. 54, no. 1 (2012), pp. 1–12.

Suggestions for further study

At various points in this book I have recommended other books and studies that will help you to follow up a subject.

In respect of accessible accounts of the life of Jesus, I would like to add the following:

- Sean Freyne, *Jesus, a Jewish Galilean: A New Reading of the Jesus Story* (London/New York: T. & T. Clark, 2004).
- Tom Wright, *Simply Jesus: A New Vision of Who he Was, What he Did, and Why he Matters* (London: SPCK, 2011).

And finally, I would mention an inspirational account of the struggle to live out the call of Jesus to love the enemy and to be a peacemaker:

- Elias Chacour, *Blood Brothers* (Grand Rapids, MI: Baker, 2003; original 1984).